Meditation
FOR RELAXATION

Meditation

FOR RELAXATION

60 MEDITATIVE PRACTICES TO REDUCE STRESS, CULTIVATE CALM, AND IMPROVE SLEEP

Adam O'Neill

ALTHEA
PRESS

Cover and Interior Designer: Darren Samuel
Art Producer: Sue Bischofberger
Editor: Nana K. Twumasi
Production Editor: Melissa Edeburn
Illustration © 2019 Darren Samuel
Author Photography © 2019 Anya Woods-O'Neill

ISBN: Print 978-1-64152-395-0 | eBook 978-1-64152-396-7

Contents

Introduction **vi**

The Meditative State **1**

PART I: Cultivate Calm and Relaxation **19**

PART II: Release Stress **61**

PART III: Drift Off to Sleep **103**

RESOURCES 144   REFERENCES 145

INDEX 149

Introduction

Welcome to *Meditation for Relaxation*. This book can change your life, if you let it. That's not hyperbole. Meditation has been around for thousands of years, and its benefits have been documented, studied, and researched for half a century. The teachings of ancient Hindu and Buddhist texts and the many recent rigorous research studies agree: Meditation can improve your quality of life.

Although meditation has religious roots, the practice of meditation is not inherently religious, and it will not conflict with your faith or beliefs (or lack thereof). If you are new to this practice, think of it like this: As much as we rely on them for the amazing things we do and fascinating lives we lead, our minds also tend to control us. Our minds manage, often poorly, how we experience and react to the world. Chronic stress, anxiety, depression, and the myriad side effects of those conditions, including sleep deprivation, are often exacerbated by the ruminations, fantasies, and obsessions of our minds. Meditation lets us take some space from these thoughts and fixations in order to find more peace, clarity, awareness, and calm.

Meditation has been a part of my life since before I was born. My mother is a certified yoga teacher who has been teaching yoga and meditation for more than 40 years. She meditated and practiced prenatal yoga when she was pregnant with me. My mom practiced yoga, chanted, and talked about yogic philosophy and the benefits of meditation so frequently that my brother and I groaned and grumbled. To her credit, she never imposed her yoga or meditation practices on us, though she did encourage us to try them. When I was a high school and college athlete, Mom always told me to "use the breath," her shorthand for tuning in to the present moment, to improve my mental preparation, focus, and performance. Despite her influence, I didn't find my own authentic connection to yoga or meditation until I was in my midtwenties.

At the time I was doing physical therapy for sciatica related to a back injury. At the beginning of a session, the physical therapist asked me to do a stretch I immediately recognized as a yoga pose. The therapist asked me to do another, and then another, each position nearly identical to the yoga poses with which I'd grown up. These stretches were a revelation: Had I been doing them all along, they probably would have given me the flexibility, strength, and body awareness to have avoided my injury. If only I'd listened to you, Mom!

In the following six months I thought a lot about why I hadn't practiced yoga and meditation. I thought about my brother, my dad, my uncles, friends, and teammates—all of the men in my life who could greatly benefit from yoga and meditation, but who would likely never try them. It eventually occurred to me that the word "yoga" as it was used in mainstream culture was not fully resonating with men. A lightbulb went on. In the 12 years since, yoga and meditation have become the primary focus of my professional life. Along with my cofounder Robert Sidoti, I've been committed to making yoga more appealing and accessible to populations worldwide (not just men) with our company YFM: Yoga. Fitness. Mindfulness., where we offer video-streaming content via our website YFM.tv as well as our popular Broga® ("yoga for bros") classes. The best part of my job? Hearing from our members about the profound impact yoga and meditation have had on their lives.

One of the most powerful revelations meditation can bring you, and the one I hope to share with you here, is that *you do not have to feel as stressed, anxious, worried, or exhausted as you do.* As you engage with the practices in this book, you'll develop a healthier relationship with your thoughts. By detaching from your thoughts, you'll begin to let go of the obsessions and worries that often bog you down and stress you out. You may see shifts in how you go about your day, resulting in reduced stress. After practicing meditation for several consecutive days, or weeks, you may feel improvements in your general state of mind, including greater calm, freedom, control, and better-quality sleep.

I know meditation can feel a little awkward, uncomfortable, and challenging at first. This is totally normal and understandable. I share some tips to help reduce friction as you get started, but here is the number one secret: You simply have to give yourself the time to meditate. Make time for it, commit to the practices, and everything else will follow.

Let's get started.

The Meditative State

Before we dive into the practice, let's take a moment to understand medi-tation and its proven benefits for relaxation, stress reduction, and sleep. I encourage you to spend some time with this section. In it, you'll find impor-tant context, tips for getting the most out of this book, and the essential core principles of meditation. Without this foundational understanding, you may find the meditation practices frustrating or confusing, and that's the last thing I want. Having a basic comprehension of the simple principles of meditation will only make the practices and your experience more rewarding.

Do you ever feel like you need an extra hour? Better yet, an extra day? Do you feel like life is moving faster than you want? Like it's difficult to keep up? Or like you can keep up, but there isn't enough time to do the things you actually *want* to do? Are you worried about the future? Do you feel anxious, uneasy, exhausted, or a combination of all three?

If any of these feelings resonate with you, don't worry—they're all too common in our modern culture. We are continually pushed by our ingrained personal expectations and mounting external responsibilities. And though we like to believe that the television shows we binge-watch and the devices we're attached to help us relax, they only serve to entertain us (at best) and add to our overwhelm.

This perpetual cycle, which I call "over-stress, under-rest," often leaves us too awake to sleep, but too tired to do anything productive. In fact, chronic stress and sleep deprivation are now epidemics in many countries around the world. This cycle can lead to major health problems, addictions, and troubled relationships. If we don't make changes, we could be left with years of blurry, mindless repetition. But life doesn't have to be this way.

As you will learn in the coming chapters, simple, accessible meditation practices can help you relax, find calm, and improve the depth and duration of your sleep.

Research continues to show that meditation offers significant benefits to our mental and physical health by creating a positive cycle of improvements— better sleep leads to a better mood, leads to higher emotional resilience, leads to feeling more relaxed, leads to better sleep. This section reveals the proven benefits you can expect to experience by practicing the meditations in this book. Improvement in any one of these areas can have a substantial long-term impact on your quality of life.

Stress Reduction

Multiple research studies show that meditation reduces stress. A 2014 analysis by *JAMA Internal Medicine* representing more than 3,500 participants in multiple studies found that regular meditation produced improvements in several types of negative psychological stress, including anxiety, depression, and pain. Moreover, a 2013 study at the University of Wisconsin–Madison concluded that an eight-week meditation program reduced stress-induced inflammation in participants. Additionally, a 2014 analysis of more than 600 research papers representing nearly 1,300 participants concluded that meditation reduces stress, especially among those with the highest levels. And that's just the beginning.

Improved Sleep

Our stores of melatonin, the hormone associated with restful sleep, are most depleted by stress. Meditation both reduces stress and assists the natural melatonin production mechanisms of the body, meaning it can help you fall asleep faster and sleep longer. One 2012 study from a team at Rutgers University found that meditation increased melatonin levels in some participants by 300 percent.

Restful Meditation

Anecdotal evidence has shown that even short periods of meditation can have the hormonal and neurological benefits of two to three times the same amount of sleep—meaning it's possible for you to meditate for 20 minutes and feel as rested as you would after an hour of sleep, without the grogginess. This isn't to say that you can meditate *instead* of sleeping, of course (though some dedicated practitioners report needing less sleep as a result of meditating consistently over long periods of time). You still need your sleep, but with short bursts of meditation you can experience many of the benefits of deep sleep *and* get better sleep (when you aren't meditating).

Heightened Awareness

In addition to heightening your awareness of what is happening in the present moment outside of your body and mind, meditation helps tune your awareness to the sensations, emotions, and sources of stress and tension within your body and mind. This heightened awareness has many immediate and long-term benefits.

For example, if you have undesirable habits that are triggered by physical or emotional stress, meditation will help you develop sensitivity to both the stressor and your default response. This sensitivity can give you more control over your choices. For instance, when you feel the 3 p.m. slump, you can choose to not have that extra cup of coffee in the afternoon. Or you can pause in the evening and decide not to have a bowl of chocolate ice cream before bed. Both of these mindful choices would improve the quality and duration of your sleep, thus reducing your stress. Heightened awareness also increases sensations of joy, gratitude, and wonder. The more aware you are of the good things around and within you, the more you will enjoy them.

Reduced Blood Pressure

The American Heart Association reviewed a number of studies on meditation and its effects on blood pressure and discovered some evidence suggesting that meditation can help reduce blood pressure. There is a known physiological response to stress reduction, which we know meditation supports. However, meditation should not be viewed as a primary method for treating hypertension. If you are concerned about high blood pressure, discuss it with your doctor. In the meantime, know that meditation won't cause any harm, and it may actually be meaningfully helpful.

Equanimity

As we go about our busy days, it's inevitable to encounter people and situations that make us feel annoyed, frustrated, angry, sad, jealous, or irritated. But what if you could react differently to these triggers—or not react at all? What if you simply observed the wrongdoing, the inconvenience, the irritant but didn't internalize it? Chances are, that moment—and the subsequent moments throughout your day—would be much more pleasant for everyone involved.

Practicing meditation helps you develop the ability to recognize that the emotional stressor or trigger is not the reaction. They are separate, and therefore your reaction is under your control—you can choose to let something stress you out, or not. You'll never be able to change all of the crazy stuff that happens in life, but you can change how it impacts you. Developing this ability through regular meditation helps you alleviate stress in real time so you can save your energy for more important and more enjoyable things.

YOUR THOUGHTS DO NOT DEFINE YOU

From the moment we have consciousness, we begin trying to figure out the world around us: where to find food, how to get love, how to feel safe. As we whiz through our formative years, we're trained to think "faster," "deeper," and "harder" to solve the problems of life. By the time we become adults, most of us have a codependent relationship with our thoughts, in which our thoughts have too much power over our state of being. We come to believe that our thoughts are true and that they define us. Meditation helps us untangle this relationship.

A Busy Mind

Whether we notice it or not, our minds are constantly whirring away, trying to make sense of complex emotions, to create order, and to get approval and praise from others or running through completely made-up scenarios and worrying over them obsessively.

As this sequence carries on, we fly through each passing moment, completely missing the fact that it is the *only* moment in which we actually live, that each moment is profoundly rich with sensation and space and calm and insight. By living in our thoughts, we also often miss out on the experience of living in our bodies, of experiencing what it feels like to be alive, in this moment, right now.

Meditation Is Not...

You may have certain images in your head about what meditation looks like, who can do it, and what it's all about. I encourage you to let go of any preconceptions you have about meditation. (I'm not going to ask you to try to levitate.)

You do not need to be a certain type of person, wear any specific type of clothing, travel to the Himalayas, chant, or pray in order to meditate. You only need to give yourself the time suggested for each practice and then follow the process.

Meditation is powerful, but it will not hurt you. Your experience will vary from day to day and practice to practice. Some days or practices will feel great, and others will feel like a real struggle. But if you stick with it, you can find a path to relaxation, calm, and peace you may not have traveled before, and it can become one that you value immensely.

Meditation helps us recognize that our thoughts are creations of our brains, that we can observe them with objectivity, and that we can choose how they impact us.

Engaging with the Present Moment

Meditation is the practice of quieting your thoughts for the purpose of becoming completely aware of the present moment. As you rekindle your relationship with the present, you can live in it more fully, with greater awareness, deeper sensitivity, and more intention.

As you begin exploring these practices, you will discover that your thoughts are just your thoughts, creations of your mind, and that you have the ability to let them pass and instead exist with complete attention in the present moment.

In my own practice, I've identified eight guiding principles of meditation. Each principle below is based on my experience, but I give a lot of credit to Jon Kabat-Zinn, one of the leading teachers in mindfulness meditation, who has written extensively on meditation and inspired me in my journey. Feel free to come back to this section to get grounded before you begin a practice or to check in after meditating to see how these principles guided your practice and how they are showing up in your life (because they will start showing up, over and over).

Patience. As you begin meditating, you'll find that your brain will work very hard to get your attention: *What was that sound? Did I turn off the heat? I wonder what Joe is doing.* This will happen often, and it's completely normal. You may also start noticing physical distractions—your leg might fall asleep, or you may want to fidget to get more comfortable—as well as external distractions, like a bird chattering or the doorbell ringing.... Your mind will be tempted to follow each distraction, and this might frustrate you. Be patient. Acknowledge the distractions, let them go (unless your leg is falling asleep, in which case you should adjust), and bring your attention back to your practice. Enter into each meditation with a mind-set of patience, so you are ready to accept whatever arises, including your own frustrations or doubts.

Acceptance. Acceptance goes hand in hand with patience and means that you're fully accepting whatever you're experiencing, whether it is an external sound or sensation or an internal thought or emotion. With practice, you'll begin to accept *all* that you experience, in meditation and beyond. In many ways, acceptance *is* meditation.

Nonjudgmental Awareness. One of the most important principles of meditation is the concept of nonjudgmental awareness. Our minds are almost always judging. *That was rude, this tastes good, it's too cold, I'm overweight, she's good looking,* and on and on. We compare, categorize, and label in an effort to organize and understand the world: It can be difficult to turn off this judging impulse, but it's extremely worthwhile. Meditation encourages us to practice nonjudgmental awareness, which allows us to put space between our experience and our reaction so we can simply observe what's happening. As new thoughts, sounds, smells, and sensations clamor for our attention, we are simply aware—without labeling, without judging.

Compassion. We are born with an innate capacity for compassion, and it continues to develop as we grow. We learn that if we pull hair or hit, it hurts another person. We learn that some people are less fortunate than we are. We learn that making other people feel good makes us feel good. Meditation is powerful for compassion. It strips away our fears and pride and emotional reactions, revealing that under the surface we are simply human beings. As you experience this stripping away more frequently through meditation, you may begin to feel a liberating humility that manifests as a deep reservoir of compassion for yourself and for others.

Forgiveness. When you aren't as easily frustrated by events, circumstances, or even your own thoughts, when you learn to accept all things outside of your control, without judgment and with compassion for yourself and others, you'll find it's much easier to let go of grudges and practice forgiveness. Forgiveness can take you even deeper into the principles of meditation, and we'll explore this concept with several practices in this book.

Trust. As you explore a state of being that quiets your thoughts, your mind will try all sorts of tricks to get back in the driver seat. You may get a sudden surge of fear, or skepticism, or irritability. Sometimes the thoughts or emotions that rise up will be very strong, perhaps even strong enough to pull you away. That's okay. It's all part of the process. But meditation is a practice that's worthy of your trust. If something pulls you out of it, trust that it is worthwhile to go back in. Trust in what it's doing for you. Trust that it's always there for you. Over time, this trust will help you get more from your meditation practice.

Nonattachment. We tend to be precious about our things, our thoughts, our ideas, and our preferences. We get attached to the outcomes we want. Nonattachment reminds you not to hold onto anything; that all things and experiences and beings are impermanent. This mind-set helps us in our practice and as we go about our daily lives.

Nonstriving. This idea can be challenging for some people, especially those who are perfectionists or overachievers. We've been conditioned to identify with our goals and to approach things for the purpose of achieving or getting ahead. The principle of nonstriving reminds us to simply observe, without desire or intention to accomplish anything. The purpose of each meditation practice is just to bring your awareness to the present moment. That's all you need to do.

Stopping to meditate can feel absurd when there are so many other things to do. But not making time for ourselves is a big part of the problem we're addressing here, a big part of why you might feel so anxious or have trouble sleeping. If it's helpful, instead of thinking of meditation as taking time away from other, "more important," things you need to do, think of meditation as the superpower that enables you to be more focused, more clear-headed, and more efficient throughout the rest of your day.

MBSR and MBCT

If you're still unsure about the healing benefits of meditation for body and mind, consider these two medical treatment methodologies that incorporate the principles of meditation and mindfulness. The effectiveness and popularity of these treatments demonstrate the incredible research-based results of meditation. If either of these therapies sounds right for you or someone you love, I encourage you to do more research.

Mindfulness-Based Stress Reduction (MBSR)

MBSR was developed, in the 1970s, by Jon Kabat-Zinn, one of the first researchers to bring rigorous scientific study to the field of mindfulness meditation, for the purpose of treating a range of conditions that were difficult to address in conventional medical settings. An eight-week workshop, MBSR combines mindfulness meditation, body awareness, and yoga to help individuals reduce stress and relax. MBSR programs have been introduced to hospitals around the world, major corporations, and even the U.S. Congress. MBSR is practiced as a complementary medicine, and some form of MBSR education has been introduced to most medical schools. Thousands of MBSR instructors have been certified and lead programs around the United States.

Mindfulness-Based Cognitive Therapy (MBCT)

MBCT is an eight-week group therapy program developed, in the early 1990s, by the esteemed mindfulness research team of John Teasdale, Zindel Segal, and Mark Williams. The program builds on the MBSR method developed by Kabat-Zinn. Combining conventional psychotherapy methods with mindfulness practices, MBCT was originally developed to treat individuals with depression. (MBSR is more general.) Biochemical factors play a significant role in depression, but so do thoughts and an individual's relationship with them. Using mindfulness meditation methods, MBCT helps patients observe their thoughts as impermanent creations ("events") of their brains, instead of true representations of "self." MBCT has been found to be effective for depression and is also being studied for a variety of other health applications, including diabetes and cancer.

All meditation is built on the same basic principles, but there are numerous types. You don't need to know the specific type you're doing to reap the benefits, but I include seven types to help you build your practice. I encourage you to try a few to find the approaches that feel best to you.

Mindfulness. Mindfulness is being aware—i.e., "mindful"—of what you are doing, thinking, feeling, and experiencing in the present moment. There are many approaches to mindfulness meditation, including scanning the sensations of your body, focusing on your breath, or simply becoming openly aware of all that is happening in and around you. This meditation can be done seated, lying down, or walking.

Vipassana. Believed to have been developed by the Buddha, Vipassana is very similar to general mindfulness in that it uses the breath and cultivates awareness. This type of meditation is unique in that it teaches us to recognize thoughts, sounds, and sensations by making note of them as they pass with phrases such as "I am hearing…," "I am thinking…," or "I am feeling…"

Phrases and Affirmations. This type of meditation involves repeating certain phrases to help focus the mind. These phrases tend to be simple and affirming, such as: "I am here." "I am alive." "My word is good." "I am peaceful." By focusing on the inherent meaning in the words and repeating them consistently, we can cultivate compassion, equanimity, forgiveness, gratitude, joy, confidence, clarity, or other states of mind.

Focus and Concentration. Many meditations use a focal point for our attention. This focal point can be internal, such as a specific sensation related to the breath or a thought, or external, such as looking at a particular object or listening to a specific sound. Focusing on a candle flame, listening to chimes or the sound of rain, or holding mental focus on a particular idea are all forms of this type of meditation.

Chanting. Chants (also known as mantras in some traditions) use the breath and sound to create a real-time physical sensation in your head, throat, and chest through the vibration of your vocal cords. This immersive experience helps bring us into deep connection with the present moment. Most religions and many types of meditations call for some form of chanting. Whereas phrases and affirmations often have direct and clear meaning ("I am here"), chants may use words or phrases from another language, are often ancient and handed down through generations, and are typically recited aloud in large groups. Chants are used by monks in monasteries and congregations in churches. In chanting, the sounds of the words are as impactful as the meaning of the words.

Tonglen. Tonglen comes from a Tibetan tradition and encourages using the breath as the vehicle for specific energetic exchange. For instance: inhaling peace and tranquility, exhaling stress and tension.

Visualization. Visualization meditations, often called "guided" or "nidra" meditations in the yogic traditions, are guided by words in a book, in audio recordings, or spoken by teacher. By imagining landscapes, environments, and scenarios, visualization meditations can help cultivate desirable mind-sets, emotional states, beliefs, and habits. They can also be effective in guiding athletes in performance and addressing trauma. This book presents several guided meditations.

You don't need anything other than an open mind to meditate. But here are some tips that may make the practice easier. Flip back to this section when you find yourself frustrated or discouraged about your practice.

Meditation Is for Anyone. In yoga, we often hear people say, "Oh, I can't do yoga, I'm not flexible at all." This excuse baffles me because it means people are assuming that what is a *result* of the practice (flexibility) is actually a *prerequisite* for even trying it, which is simply not true. A similar principle applies to meditation. If you are someone who thrives on busyness and self-identifies as anxious, exhausted, or stressed, then you may think that meditation isn't for you. In fact, trying meditation would be a *great* idea for you. Meditation can help anyone find space and calm in their minds and lives. It also reveals that your self-concepts ("I'm too busy") are simply thoughts—and you no longer have to believe them.

You Have the Time. Even a few short minutes of meditation are better than none. I know it can be difficult at first to prioritize something that has the appearance of not being "productive." But the truth is that meditation is extremely productive, perhaps one of the *most* productive things you can do with 5 or 10 minutes. Make the time. You don't need much. Try putting your next practice on your calendar or setting an alarm on your phone. Commit and follow through—I know you can find 5 to 10 minutes somewhere in your day.

Create the Space. You can meditate anywhere—on the train, in a plane, in a hotel lobby, in a conference room. But it can be helpful, especially in the beginning, to try to reduce distractions. You don't need a special chair or cushion, but you do want to be physically comfortable. Less noise makes it easier to focus at first, so find the quietest place available. You can also listen to soothing ambient music on headphones or speakers to drown out any background noise. At home, find a place where you can have some privacy and get comfortable, and make that place your dedicated meditation spot.

Unplug. Put your phone in airplane mode (unless you need it for music with headphones, in which case you should turn off all notifications). Turn off your computer or put it in sleep mode. Turn off any alarms that may disrupt you. Sometimes the present moment includes distractions out of our control, which can be challenging but which are important to accept. One area under our control is our digital lives, so unplug and put devices away before you settle in.

Get Comfortable. Wherever you are, try to find a comfortable position. You can be seated on a chair, on a bench, or on a cushion on the floor. Try to find a position in which you won't get sore after a few minutes and in which your legs won't fall asleep. If you're in a public place, position yourself so that you aren't in the way, to avoid disruptions. If sitting won't work for you for some reason, lying flat on your back *can* work, but you run the risk of falling asleep. Ideally, you want to be comfortable but not so comfortable that you doze off.

All You Have to Do Is Try. Remember this advice as you start your practice: You can't "fail" at meditation. Sure, you may struggle with it, but experienced practitioners also struggle. Go easy on yourself. There are no rules about meditation, so don't be too rigid about it. Even 30 seconds of meditation can be worthwhile. Just keep carving out the time each practice calls for and trying to focus your mind on the present moment. Over time, you'll find an approach and a rhythm that work for you. As long as you try, you will experience the benefits of meditation.

How Will I Know If Meditation Works?

Remember that the purpose of meditation is to cultivate clear awareness of the present moment. As you do this, you will begin to see your thoughts as just thoughts, not truths, and to start to find space between stressors and your responses. Through these practices, there are an infinite number of ways your meditation practice will help you in your life. If you begin to notice that you take more deep breaths throughout the day, or that you let thoughts go instead of gripping onto them, or that you're generally more relaxed, calm, or getting better sleep, you will know that meditation is working.

MAKE THIS BOOK WORK FOR YOU

This book is *your* book, designed to help you with *your* meditation practice. Meditation practices are independent one from another, so you do not need to attempt them in any particular order. Find the practices you like the most and repeat them as often as you'd like. Or start out by trying a new meditation for every practice until you settle on an approach that works best for you.

Think of the meditations that follow as the first steps down an open-ended, fascinating path of self-discovery. They are specifically designed to reduce stress, promote relaxation, and improve the quality of your sleep. But you may experience even more significant shifts. Don't shy away from them. Continue on your path. Keep exploring.

Stretch Yourself and Your Practice

The practices in the book range in duration—some are 5 minutes, some are 25 minutes. I encourage you to try all of them. You won't be able to know which ones work best for you by simply reading them. You have to *do* them. Start out with the shorter practices and work your way up. As you become more comfortable, try longer and longer practices.

Accept Frustration

You will almost certainly experience some frustration or restlessness with your practice from time to time (maybe even every time). Remember that these emotions are products of your mind. Observe them and let them go. If they are so strong that you find it impossible to get back into your meditation, it's okay to step away. But don't let that time be the last time you ever try meditation, and don't hold onto any feelings of frustration. Let them go, regroup, make another time, review the principles on page 7, and try again. As I mentioned before, even the most experienced meditators experience intense psychological and emotional resistance at times. This resistance is normal. All you can do is accept it for what it is.

Let the Journey Begin

As is no doubt evident by now, I truly believe in the power of meditation. I'm thrilled to share the following practices with you, and I sincerely hope that you will find them beneficial. If you are new to meditation, refer back to this chapter often for encouragement and a reminder that you're on the right track.

Remember that you are embarking on a journey during which you will encounter new experiences and rediscover yourself, and the optimal outcome is finding more space, clarity, calm, and rest. This journey is worth taking.

PART I
Cultivate Calm and Relaxation

Though we often aren't aware of it, total relaxation is available to us in nearly every moment in our lives, regardless of circumstances. This option is usually obscured by our thoughts, stress, and the general busyness of our lives. If we don't have experience with intentionally accessing a state of relaxation, remembering that it's even an option can be difficult. Meditation provides a tool kit for accessing relaxation in any moment. As you become more familiar with using it, remembering that you always have a choice becomes easier. The meditations in this section are designed to help you get relaxed. As you practice them more over time, you may find that you also use them more frequently. I hope you do.

1

THE CLASSIC RESET *5 MINUTES*

This meditation is a common entry point to practice. It gives you a sense of what meditation is, and you can scale it to practices of any duration. Meditation doesn't get much simpler than this, but simple doesn't always equal easy. Be patient. Take your time. Almost all of the practices that follow build on this exercise, so I encourage you to do this one first and return to it often. Set a timer for 5 minutes and build up the duration as you get more comfortable meditating.

1. Find a comfortable seated position. You can sit cross-legged on a cushion on the floor or in a chair. Sit up straight, but don't force perfect posture.

2. Gently close your eyes or soften your gaze.

3. Without changing anything, bring your attention to your breath. Notice the expansion of your chest and abdomen on each inhale, and feel your lungs empty as you exhale.

4. Remind yourself that at this moment, you have nowhere else to be and nothing else to do.

5. On your next exhale, exhale completely, pushing all the air out of your lungs. Then allow your diaphragm to expand naturally, letting the inhale take care of itself. Repeat this series one more time.

6. Notice whether you feel a little more relaxed.

7. Now, let the breath flow naturally without doing anything to change or control it. Find a place where the breath feels the best, maybe at the tip of your nose, the back of your throat, or the bottom of your lungs. Focus your attention there.

8. For the next several minutes, keep your attention on this part of your breath.

9. As distractions arise, such as thoughts, sensations, or sounds, just notice them and let them go. Bring your attention back to the breath. You have nowhere else to be and nothing else to do.

10. Simply remain in present awareness of your breath for the next few minutes.

TIP: What does it mean to "soften your gaze"? Our eyes tend to be active all day—scanning, watching, shifting focus. The instruction to "soften your gaze" (which you'll see in many meditations in this book) simply means to direct your gaze forward and slightly down, focusing on nothing in particular; allow your eyes, eyelids, and the muscles around them to completely relax.

2

PRESENT AND COMPLETE *5 MINUTES*

Much of our stress and anxiety comes from the belief that we are somehow insufficient, inadequate, or incomplete. We tend to think that if we could just try a little bit harder, we would finally be fulfilled and worthy of complete relaxation. For this meditation, you're going to abandon that way of thinking and do the complete opposite. By holding onto the feeling of being complete, whole, and utterly perfect just the way you are in this moment, you will reset the expectations you place on yourself, and you will grow more aware of the reality of the present, achieving instant calm.

1. Find a comfortable seated position. You can sit cross-legged on a cushion on the floor or in a chair. Sit up straight, but don't force perfect posture.

2. Soften your gaze or gently close your eyes.

3. Become aware of your breath. Without trying to change or control your inhales and exhales, simply follow their natural rhythm.

4. Let any thoughts in your mind fade away as you continue to focus on your breath.

5. Spend a minute or two keeping your attention on your breath. If your mind wanders, bring it back.

6. When you're ready, over the next few breaths, begin to repeat the following words silently to yourself: On each inhale tell yourself, *I am present and complete.* On each exhale tell yourself, *I am perfect just the way I am.*

7. Repeat this for the next few minutes. As you inhale, feel the wholeness of your body, the warmth of your limbs. As you exhale, let go of any lingering stress.

8. Remain present. You are exactly where you need to be, alive and in the moment. You are complete. You do not need to do anything or become anyone else. You are perfectly yourself in this moment and in every moment. You are enough. You are good.

9. When you are ready to complete your meditation, bring your attention to your fingers. Move them gently. Slowly wiggle your toes. Gently move your limbs and tilt your head from side to side.

TIP: As you shift back into your day, bring this practice with you. Notice: Do you feel stress or anxiety building when you're around certain people, perhaps a boss or someone who has influence over your "external" life? Do you give yourself a hard time when you make a mistake at work or at home? Remember that you are always in the present moment and that you can bring your awareness back to it. There is nothing you can do about the past and the future is unknowable. In this moment you are you, perfectly adequate, present, and complete.

3

YOU CAN'T TAKE IT WITH YOU *15 MINUTES*

Whether we realize it or not, we all carry around layers of memory and emotion. Throughout our lives, we are imprinted by our personal experience, which leads us to establish certain behaviors, beliefs, biases, and automatic reactions to the world. Although our pasts are valuable chapters in the stories of our lives, the past is gone. Holding onto the past has little value to the *now*. It's impossible—and even undesirable—to erase all memories and emotional experiences, but it's important to recognize that our past does not need to continually influence our current state of being. You can learn to let go of the past by cultivating and developing an appreciation for the only moment in which we are actively alive: right now. In this meditation, you'll use a simple phrase to maintain awareness of the present moment: *I am now*. Letting go of the past is a powerful tool for relaxing into what is.

1. Find a comfortable position. You can sit cross-legged on a cushion on the floor or in a chair. Sit up straight, but don't force perfect posture.

2. Without trying to change or control your breath, observe it. Follow each inhale and exhale.

3. Let all thoughts dissolve from your mind. Say quietly out loud or in your mind, *I am now.*

4. Over the next few minutes, as you maintain a connection to your breath, observe the thoughts and sensations that arise. Without judgment, acknowledge their existence and let them pass.

5. You may find that many are memories, perhaps vague, perhaps vivid, and that they bring emotions with them.

6. As interruptions arise, either internally or externally, come back to your breath and repeat, *I am now.*

4

WEIGHTLESS *10 MINUTES*

Have you ever marveled at the soaring, hovering, and swooping of birds and insects? The idea of flying across vast distances, seeing for miles, gliding effortlessly through the air, is awe-inspiring for us land-bound humans. In our day-to-day lives, we're often so close to the sources of our stress and anxiety that we cannot see them with any space or perspective. In this meditation, you'll use your "sense" of what flying might feel like in order to explore a liberating shift in perspective. Try driving to a place with a nice view and doing the meditation while sitting in your car. This meditation also works well as a walking meditation.

1. Find a comfortable seated position. You can sit cross-legged on a cushion on the floor or in a chair. Sit up straight, but don't force perfect posture.

2. Connect with your breath, finding awareness of each inhale and exhale. For a few breaths, simply connect to the expansion of your lungs when you inhale and the relaxation of your abdomen when you exhale.

3. When you are ready, soften your gaze. If you are seated, you can gently close your eyes.

4. Envision a bird with large wings soaring above you. Visualize how it looks out at the distant horizon and occasionally down to you, a tiny speck on the terrain below.

5. Now, see through the bird's eyes. Looking down and ahead, you see a winding river and a road through a forest.

6. You're gliding effortlessly, with the wind rushing past your head and under your wings. Your body feels supported by the air. You feel free and secure.

7. A warm gush of air rises up from below, lifting you up and propelling you forward.

8. You are not trying to get anywhere. You're simply flying, aware of everything you pass but unaffected by it.

9. Perhaps next you see a farm, or a city, or a mountain range. Do not try to paint the picture of what you see next, simply let it come as you continue to soar along.

10. When you are ready to return home, imagine gently tilting your body to circle around and flying back the way you came.

11. As you get closer to where you started, begin to bring your attention back to your breath, to your body, to your surroundings.

12. Take time to reconnect with your body, slowly moving your fingers and toes.

13. Notice how you feel as you come out of this meditation and return to your day. Have you gained some perspective? Do some of the worries and stresses you were feeling before now seem smaller and less important—as though you can soar over them without getting pulled down?

TIP: Walking meditations can be done anywhere, but a quiet trail in the forest or in a park is the best setting. As an immersive, full-body experience, walking offers a rich variety of sensations and sounds in each moment: the steps of your feet, the swing of your arms, the feel of the sun or the wind. If you are doing a visualization meditation while walking, you can't close your eyes, but you can soften your gaze to keep your attention on the meditation. Your body and peripheral vision will naturally keep you on the trail.

5

CANDLE FLAME *10 MINUTES*

There are many ways to cultivate your awareness of the present moment. One simple approach is to establish a visual focal point where you can rest your eyes and focus your mind. In this meditation, you'll practice the technique by watching the flame of a candle. Any type of candle will work, but one with a bigger flame and little or no scent (which can become distracting) is preferable.

1. Light your candle. Lower the lights so the candle becomes the only light in the room.

2. Find a comfortable seated position in which the candle flame is at or slightly below eye level. Sit up straight, but don't force perfect posture.

3. Close your eyes. Without trying to change or control your inhales and exhales, follow their natural rhythm for the next several breaths. Connect to the feeling of being alive, comfortable, and relaxed.

4. Gently open your eyes, soften your gaze, and look at the flame. Don't strain your eyes to stare intensely, and don't focus on any specific part of the flame. Just find a soft visual connection with it.

5. As you settle in, begin to notice the striations of color, where they're distinct and where they blend. You may see whites and blues, oranges, and reds. You may even see greens and violets. Try not to label the colors as you see them. Simply observe.

6. Notice how the light around the flame dances and evolves, how the shape of the flame is always moving and changing, yet never goes out.

7. Keep your gaze on the flame, maintaining connection with your breath for the next several minutes.

8. As thoughts arise, observe them, let them go, and return your focus to the candle and your breath.

TIP: Blinking will happen naturally. You aren't trying to force your eyes to stay open or maintain intense focus. Simply relax and observe.

6

SMOOTH TUNES *10 TO 25 MINUTES*

Music is powerful. It can entertain, inspire, change your mood, trigger strong memories, spark you to dance or move your body, and even modulate the behavior of entire crowds. In this meditation, you will use music as a focal point. Because you'll be listening in a different way than you typically do, it's best to choose music you're not already familiar with. That way, you can't anticipate what you'll hear next. You can find lots of free and accessible meditation music tracks online. Listen to a few options to find one you like.

1. You can do this meditation while seated on a cushion or in a chair, lying down, or walking.

2. Play your selected meditation music track on headphones or speakers.

3. Bring awareness to your breath, exhaling completely. Follow the natural sensation of your breath, coming in and going out.

4. Maintaining a steady natural breath, without trying to change or control it, turn your attention to the music.

5. Notice the notes, tones, rhythms, melodies, and harmonies in the music. Become aware of the music without trying to anticipate or analyze it. Don't judge or describe it. Simply receive it as it comes. Observe the sensations in your ears and in your body.

6. As thoughts attempt to interrupt your focus, acknowledge them, let them pass, and return your attention to the music.

7. You are not attempting to think about the music or even to "enjoy" it per se. You're simply accepting it, hearing it as it comes, and being present with the experience of the sounds.

8. If you find yourself getting distracted, return to your breath for a few cycles before focusing on the music again.

9. When you are ready to transition out of this meditation, slowly move your fingers and toes. Take a couple of deep breaths. Bring your attention back to where you are, any other sounds that surround you, and the sensations in your body. When you are ready, turn off the music.

TIP: When searching for the right track or album, be sure to specify "meditation" music in your search. You'll want something that is atmospheric, instrumental, and relaxing. Lyrics tend to be too distracting, as do songs with a high tempo or strong beat.

7

THE SOUND OF OM *5 MINUTES*

Om or *aum* is an ancient, sacred sound found in Hinduism and Buddhism. It is believed to be the sound of all creation, the sound of the universe. It is often used in preparation for prayer as well as at the beginning and end of yoga practices. If you are concerned about religious conflict, check with your spiritual leader. But for many, the sound *om* has a secular value, like meditation itself. The vibration of your voice repeating *om* offers a soothing focal point for meditation. Here, you will meditate with the sound of *om* for 5 minutes. Keep in mind, listening to the sound of *om* can be relaxing, but the real benefit comes from creating the sound yourself.

1. Before beginning, experiment with making the sound. Slowly take in a full inhale. Open your mouth fully and as you exhale, make a sound that starts with "OOOHHHH" and then, slowly closing your mouth, changes to "MMmmmm." Try this for a few breaths. Go slowly. Don't extend the "Ohm" for so long that you're gasping for breath at the end. Practice even inhales and exhales as you continue making the sound.

2. Don't try to find any particular pitch or change the frequency of your voice. Whatever naturally comes out when you make the sound is perfect.

3. Find a comfortable seated position. You can sit cross-legged on a cushion on the floor or in a chair. Sit up straight, but don't force perfect posture.

4. Become aware of your breath, following each inhale and exhale for several cycles.

5. When you are ready, begin making the sound of *om* on each exhale. It may take a little while to find a comfortable rhythm, and you may begin to lengthen your inhales and exhales.

6. Maintain the quality of your breath, keeping your inhales slow and complete and your exhales even across the entire sound of *om*.

7. As you make the sound, maintain awareness. Notice the sensation in your head, throat, chest, lungs, and belly. Sense the vibration of the sound inside and outside of yourself.

8. Try to hear the sound as though you aren't making it. Try to "be" the sound and become totally immersed in it.

9. Notice the tiny variations in sound quality and consistency as you keep chanting.

10. Notice any thoughts or distractions that arise, then let them go and return your attention to the sound.

11. After about 5 minutes, or whenever you are ready, conclude this meditation after a long *om* by returning to your normal breathing. Take a moment to scan your body and your mind. Take a deep breath and exhale completely. Move your fingers and toes, perhaps stretch your whole body, and notice how you feel.

TIP: If *om* is entirely new to you, search for an audio track online to get used to what it sounds like.

8

WALLFLOWER *5 MINUTES*

In this meditation, we're going to use a visual focal point on a wall as an anchor for cultivating awareness—a practice that can be challenging for many, myself included, in part because it seems so strange at first. But if you can suspend your skepticism and approach this meditation with intention, you'll find it worthwhile. What you're looking at is not as important as the act of setting your gaze.

1. Find a spot in your home, office, or outside where you can comfortably sit a few feet away from a wall. The wall can be plain, textured, or colored. It doesn't matter. You may prefer a plain, smooth wall or one with some visual interest.

2. Find a comfortable seated position across from your chosen wall. You can sit cross-legged on a cushion on the floor or in a chair. Sit up straight, but don't force perfect posture.

3. Set your gaze on the wall at a comfortable height in your line of sight. Don't look too far up or too far down the wall.

4. Softly focus on the surface of the wall. Don't try to stare "through" it. Don't strain your eyes.

5. Bring your awareness to your breath, following each inhale and exhale for 5 or 6 cycles.

6. With your focus set on the wall, continue to breathe in a relaxed, natural pattern.

7. You may find that your eyes want to dart around or focus intently on one thing. Our eyes always want to interpret the world and pay attention to what our minds think is important. The purpose here is to maintain

a consistent, soft focus, remaining completely aware of the present moment. If your eyes move, bring them back. If your mind begins to wander or asks *What am I doing?* or says *This is boring*, simply come back to your focal point. It may help to say *I am looking* over and over in your mind. If distractions pull you away from your focus, come back to your breath.

8. Remain a passive observer in the present moment. Observe the sensations in your body, what your eyes want to do, the interaction between your mind and your breath, and the thoughts that clamor for your attention.

9. When the meditation feels complete, softly close your eyes. Take several slow, deep breaths. Allow your breathing to return to normal and slowly open your eyes.

10. Once you come out of this meditation, notice whether your eyes are more selective about where they focus, and whether your mind is calmer in its reaction to visual stimuli.

9

PET TONIC *5 TO 10 MINUTES*

Spending time observing another life, in all of its details and subtle behaviors, is a simple way to cultivate humility, compassion, and wisdom. We experience these qualities when we spot animals in nature and when we form bonds with our pets. As with most meditations, the approach here is to establish a focal point for your mind. Choose any pet of which you are fond (either yours or a friend's) and enlist the animal to help you. This meditation brings your attention and awareness out of your own mind and onto another life.

1. Find a comfortable seated position on a cushion on the floor, in a chair, on the couch, or on a bed near a trusted pet.

2. For the next several minutes, give your undivided attention to this animal. Pet it, hold it, or simply look at it.

3. Let your breath flow naturally. Connect to it as an anchor if your mind starts to wander.

4. The intention here is to be completely present with this other life-form, to respect and marvel at its existence and presence.

5. Observe the pet's color, texture, and contours. Focus on its breathing and subtle movements.

6. Connect to the inherent trust between you and this animal. Marvel at the connection you share, in this moment, right now, and in all moments.

7. Consider how the life you are observing is precious, amazing, powerful, and fragile. Consider how this is also true of your own life.

8. To conclude this meditation, close your eyes and take 3 slow, deep breaths, then allow your breathing to return to normal. Take a moment to connect with your pet as you normally would—with a pat on the head or a scratch behind the ears. As you return to your day, note how deeply appreciating and connecting with another life makes *you* feel.

TIP: If your pet gets up and leaves during this practice, you can either continue the practice, holding onto the focus and spirit of the meditation on your own, or turn it into a walking meditation and follow the pet around.

VARIATION: This practice can be equally powerful with another person. Try it with a sleeping baby or child or even with a willing friend or partner. Without speaking, observe the shape and color and living presence of the other person. Touching is optional.

10

RAINFALL *10 MINUTES*

> *"The sound of rain needs no translation."*
> —*Zen proverb*

The sound of rain has a calming, soothing, and rejuvenating effect. For this meditation, you can either wait for a rainy day or find an extended audio track of rain online (lots of free options are available). The intention of this practice is to fully tune into the sound of the rain. Find a quiet spot (or use headphones) to prevent other sounds from interrupting.

1. If it's raining outside, find a comfortable spot where you can hear the rain well. You may even want to open a window to get closer to the sound. If you're using a recording, begin playing the track on your device. I find that headphones create a more immersive experience.

2. Find a comfortable seated position. You can sit cross-legged on a cushion on the floor or in a chair. Sit up straight, but don't force perfect posture.

3. Close your eyes and check in with your breath, following the inhale and exhale for several cycles.

4. Notice whether you are holding tension in any part of your body. If you are, let it go.

5. Quiet your mind and let go of all thoughts.

6. Bring your attention to the sound of the rain. Do not listen for anything in particular. Don't anticipate the next drop or gust of wind. Don't try to visualize the rain. Just be present with the sound. Let it fill your mind.

7. Stay with the sound of the rain for the next 10 minutes. As thoughts arise or you catch yourself losing focus, return to your breath and then to the sound.

8. You are not thinking. You are not daydreaming. You are immersing your-self in the sound, staying with the sound waves in each moment.

9. As you come to the end of this meditation, gently open your eyes. If you're listening to rain outside, notice whether your relationship with the sound changes at all as you come into your surroundings. If you're listening to a recording, gradually reduce the volume over the course of a minute or so. It can be shocking to suddenly turn it off.

TIP: The recorded sound of rain can be intense. Sometimes I need to turn it down a bit as my sensitivity to the sound increases with focus during the practice.

11

AROMATHERAPY *5 TO 10 MINUTES*

What we smell can affect us physically, emotionally, and mentally. Your sense of smell is probably more powerful than you realize. In this meditation, you'll use the power of scent to focus the mind and raise your awareness of the present moment. And don't worry, you'll only use scents that you like. Choose a favorite scented candle or essential oil. I recommend using something with a mild odor, because strong scents can quickly become overwhelming.

1. If you're using a candle, light it. If you're using an oil diffuser, add your chosen essential oil and turn it on.

2. Find a comfortable seated position or lie down flat on your back. You want to be close enough to the scent to smell it, but not so close that it's overwhelming.

3. Become aware of your breath, following each inhale and exhale for several cycles.

4. If you have any thoughts in your mind, let them all dissolve to arrive fully in the present moment.

5. Without altering your natural breathing pattern, or trying to smell, become aware of the scent as it comes to you.

6. Notice: Does the scent seem to come in waves? Is it consistent? Does it encourage you to breathe more deeply or more slowly?

7. For the next several minutes, observe how your perception of the scent changes. Does it start to fade as you become more accustomed to it? Or does it get stronger? Can you pick up different nuances of the smell?

8. Avoid straining to smell anything in particular. Avoid labeling or describing the scent. Simply stay present with it.

9. If your mind interrupts your focus with a thought, observe it, let it go, and return your focus to the scent. If you get distracted, return your focus to your breath whenever needed.

10. When the meditation feels complete, take a moment to simply reconnect with the breath, following the sensations of each inhale and exhale. Snuff out the candle or turn off the diffuser. Slowly get up and move away from the smell. Note how you feel. Going outside for a breath of fresh air may be a nice conclusion.

12

PEOPLE EVERYWHERE *15 MINUTES*

Some people (myself included) feel some anxiety in crowded spaces. Through my meditation practice, I've come to understand that this kind of anxiety results from my brain doing two things: trying to absorb all of the words, voices, and sounds around me and trying to label, sort, and prioritize all that is happening. In this meditation, we explore how stimulation influences our brains and our state of being and how we can adjust this relationship through cultivating awareness to find calm in any situation.

1. Visit a busy place, perhaps a bustling office, food court, hotel lobby, or subway stop. Find a comfortable, safe place to sit on a bench or a chair.

2. Position yourself so that you can hear everything that is going on around you.

3. Soften your gaze and find your breath. Connect with the comfort you feel within your own skin.

4. Begin to listen, but rather than listening to any one sound in particular, let each sound that reaches your ears roll past. Do not try to discern any meaning or listen more intently to any sound over another. Simply notice the sounds as they come.

5. Become aware of all the sounds and of all of their layers. Try to hear all the sounds as one single unified sound. Notice the ebbs and flows, the rises and falls, perhaps even the brief moments of silence.

6. For the next few minutes, continue to observe the sounds as they arrive at your ears. Remain observant, passive, and nonjudgmental. You may notice that certain sounds capture your attention more than others. Some may stimulate thoughts or emotions. But do not hold onto any of them. Remain open to all new sounds and let them pass. This practice is aimed at remaining calm in the chaos.

13

OBJECT OF DESIRE *15 MINUTES*

We live in a consumer culture and as a result, it's easy to become emotionally attached to the things we own. But stuff, like everything else in life, is impermanent. In this meditation, you'll practice nonattachment by focusing on a cherished physical item and letting go of the emotions around it. The item can be a letter from someone special, a souvenir, jewelry, or an heirloom. It's best to choose something you can easily hold or fit in your hand.

1. Find a comfortable seated position. You can sit cross-legged on a cushion on the floor or in a chair. Sit up straight, but don't force perfect posture. Gently hold the object in your hands.

2. For the next several minutes, direct your focus on the object. Notice its shape, colors, and textures. Does it have a scent? Does it make a noise in your hands? Is it warm or cool to your touch?

3. As you do this, your mind may wander, but bring your attention back to the object.

4. If you need to reset the practice, bring your attention to your breath, softening your gaze or even closing your eyes for a moment before returning to the object.

5. Explore the idea that what you are holding is simply an object. You create any emotion or value that it has for you. When you separate the object from the meaning you've given it, what is it?

6. To complete this meditation, gently close your eyes. Without trying to change or control it, bring your attention to your breath for 3 or 4 cycles. Take a moment to feel the gratitude you have for this object and this moment.

14

WANTING NOTHING *5 MINUTES*

A classic cartoon of the Dalai Lama shows him holding a gift from the other monks on his birthday. It's an empty box. He's smiling broadly and saying, "Wow, nothing! Just what I always wanted!" This cartoon humorously depicts the concepts of nonattachment and nonstriving. We're immensely fortunate to live in a time when nearly everything is a click away, but the allure of instant gratification can also create perpetual stress, decision fatigue, and fear of missing out or making the wrong choice. Because we are so accustomed to thinking about what we want, deciding what we want, and getting what we want quickly, this meditation can seem radical. But it offers an easy path to a state of being that is in close union with our truest selves: alive, observant, aware, and free from thinking about what we want next.

1. Find a comfortable position seated on a cushion or in a chair or lying down. If you are seated, sit up straight without forcing perfect posture.

2. Without trying to change or control your breath, bring your attention to it. Follow the sensation of each inhale and exhale.

3. Scan your body slowly from head to toe. Relax any tension in your scalp, your forehead, your neck and shoulders. Relax your chest, upper back, and lungs. Continue to move through your entire body, releasing tension.

4. Check back in with your breath.

5. For the next several minutes, say, *I am alive. I am here. I have everything I need.*

6. You may begin to experience the power in this meditation as thoughts start to arise. Your brain will "want" to be heard, will "want" attention, will "want" to do something about the statement you're making.

7. As this happens, repeat, *I am alive. I am here. I have everything I need.*

8. Return to the breath whenever you need. Continue to repeat the phrases until you feel the meditation is complete.

15

NO WORRIES *15 MINUTES*

Wanting is a strong desire for a particular experience, outcome, or thing. The other side of that coin, worry, is the concern that what you want *won't* happen or that something "bad" will happen. You can reduce worry by having a healthier, less attached relationship with what you want. In this meditation, we focus on the idea that we cannot predict the future, that the only moment that exists is this moment, right now.

1. Find a comfortable seated position. You can sit cross-legged on a cushion on the floor or on a chair. Sit up straight, but don't force perfect posture.

2. Bring awareness to your breath, following each inhale and exhale for several cycles.

3. Scan your body for tension, stress, and tightness. Relax any area that needs relaxing.

4. Return to your breath, finding a place in each inhale and exhale that feels the best. Perhaps it's in your nostrils, at the tip of your nose, or in your chest.

5. Release any lingering thoughts in your head. Let them all go.

6. Speaking softly to yourself or in your head, repeat, *I am present. Aware of this moment. Alive right now. I am free of concerns about the future.*

7. Repeat these phrases for the next 15 minutes.

8. As thoughts interrupt your concentration on the phrases, observe them with passive detachment, and let them go. You can notice where they come from, and what emotions they bring up, but don't hold onto them.

9. Return to your breath whenever you need to, and maintain a comfortable rhythm as you repeat the phrases.

16
FEELING YOUR FEELINGS *5 TO 10 MINUTES*

You know when you are angry, sad, or joyful—but have you ever stopped to examine what that emotion actually *feels* like? For example, anger can be overwhelming. It triggers a series of biochemical responses within your body that elevates heart rate, dilates blood vessels, and initiates perspiration. In moments of anger, our mind focuses on the thing that caused us to feel angry, drowning out everything else and perpetuating the emotion. If you can insert a split second of awareness when an emotion is triggered to ask yourself, *How do I feel in my body right now?* you can quickly begin to reduce the intensity of the emotion. It redirects your mind away from the emotional response. Try it the next time you feel angry, sad, or frustrated—it really works. Although you likely won't use this tool as much in moments of happiness, there's value in getting perspective on positive emotions, too. Remember: impermanence.

1. Find a comfortable seated position, either cross-legged on a cushion on the floor or in a chair, or lie down on a flat comfortable surface, such as a yoga mat.

2. Bring your attention to your breath. Follow the complete sensation of each inhale and exhale without trying to change or control it.

3. Scan your body. What are you feeling in your head? Is your face completely relaxed? Is there tightness in your neck or shoulders? Does your throat or jaw feel tense? Are your arms completely relaxed?

4. Move down through each part of your body, through your major muscle groups, heart, lungs, abdomen, and pelvic floor. Scan the muscles of your thighs and upper legs. Move down to your lower legs and into your feet.

5. As you move through your anatomy, notice how the emotion affected each part of your body. As you get in touch with the sensations, gently let go of any tension, stress, or tightness.

6. Without concentrating, simply notice how your body has been affected by the emotion.

7. As thoughts arise, notice them, and let them go. Gently notice whether your thoughts are related to the emotion that kicked off this practice, or whether the thoughts want to perpetuate the emotion.

8. To conclude this practice, return your focus to your breath. Notice the gentle sensations of each inhale and exhale. Notice how focusing on your breath makes you feel present, centered, calm, and alive. Notice how your body has reset and how your mind is now calm.

9. Without rehashing the event that created it, notice how your state of being is now totally different from the emotion you felt when you started this practice. Note how just a few minutes of reconnecting with your breath and your body completely dissolved the intensity of that emotion. As you continue to practice meditation, you may find that you become less likely to be thrown into emotional turmoil by other people or your own thoughts, and that when you are, it becomes easier to reset.

17
TRUST *15 MINUTES*

When we make our plans for tomorrow, we trust that we'll wake up in the morning. When we share a secret with a friend, we trust that they won't share it with anyone else. When a car waits for you to cross the street, you trust that the driver has his or her foot on the brake. But from a young age, we're taught that not all things are worthy of our trust, that we need to be careful. Interestingly, much of our anxiety springs from this learned lack of trust—in other people, things outside of our control, and the future. And although some amount of skepticism is required for survival, we tend to get too caught up in it. In this meditation you will abandon doubt, fear, and paranoia. From a safe, comfortable place, you'll adopt the mind-set that everything is as it seems to be and that all things are worthy of our trust. Merely introducing this concept to your mind may spark some uncomfortable vulnerability. But just for 15 minutes, we're going to relax into trust and not let our brains override our intention.

1. Find a comfortable seated position. You can sit cross-legged on the floor or in a chair. Sit up straight, but don't force perfect posture.

2. Connect with your breath, keeping the rhythm natural and fluid. Follow the sensation of each inhale and exhale for several cycles.

3. Let all preexisting thoughts dissolve from your mind. Be fully present with your breath.

4. For the next several minutes, keep your attention on your breath.

5. When you are ready, introduce the following phrase to your mind and repeat it slowly on each exhale: *I embody trust.*

6. As thoughts arise, observe them, accept them, and let them go.

7. You may find that your mind wants to introduce "yeah, buts . . ." For example, when you say, *I embody trust*, your mind says, *Yeah, but my kid is probably doing something unsavory right now.* If this happens, simply repeat the phrase, keeping your connection to the feeling complete and retaining total trust of the world, others, events, and the future. Let go of fear, skepticism, assumptions, and paranoia. Remember that those concepts are created and perpetuated by your overactive mind.

8. Without judging or analyzing, make a mental note of the thought patterns that interrupt your practice. You may identify repetitious thoughts that are unnecessary or unfounded.

9. Remain in the present moment with each breath.

10. Notice how you feel in your body and in your mind. Perhaps you feel a sense of freedom and openness? Maybe any lingering thoughts associated with fear or paranoia have dissolved? When you are ready, take 2 or 3 deep breaths and a moment to stretch your fingers, your hands, your arms, your neck and back. Stretch your legs. As you return to your day, try to hold onto this feeling of trust in your communication with others and with yourself. Try to navigate your world and your thoughts without any unfounded fear.

18

YOU ARE TRUSTWORTHY *10 MINUTES*

Just as we struggle to be trusting, we may also struggle to feel like we deserve the trust of others and of ourselves. It can be hard to believe that we are wholly trust*worthy*, but for our sense of internal harmony, the knowledge that we aren't pretending to be anything or anyone other than who we truly are is immensely important. This knowledge is one of the deepest anchor points to our sense of self and thus essential to our ability to feel calm, clear, confident, and well. In this meditation, you will focus on the completeness of your integrity, as you are, right now, in this moment.

1. Find a comfortable seated position. You can sit cross-legged on a cushion on the floor or in a chair. Sit up straight, but don't force perfect posture.

2. Soften your gaze or close your eyes.

3. Find a connection with your breath. Follow the inhale and exhale through several cycles.

4. Free your mind of thoughts. It's just you and your breath.

5. Now, without striving, feel the stability and balance in your abdomen and chest. Softly, either aloud or to yourself, repeat some affirmations about your good characteristics, such as: *I am honest, I am humble, I am encouraging, I am a good listener, I am a person of great integrity.*

6. Continue reciting affirmations, this time about the relationships that are important to you: *I am a good husband. I am a good mother. I am a good sibling.*

7. And then repeat, *My word is good. I am worthy of trust from anyone I meet.*

8. This practice presents many challenges. Your mind will want to interject judgment or qualifiers on nearly everything, such as: *Well, you could be a better husband, if you did . . .* or *You'd be a better sibling if you had . . .* and on and on.

9. The process here, as in all meditation practices, is to observe these thoughts and let them pass. Focus on embodying the *feeling* of being trustworthy. When you know that you are worthy of trust, you are calm, confident, and balanced. Stay with that quality of mind through the practice and notice how it stays with you throughout the day and in all of your interactions.

19
WATER PRESSURE *25 MINUTES*

*"Routines may include taking a warm bath or a relaxing walk in
the evening, or practicing meditation/relaxation exercises.
Psychologically, the completion of such a practice tells your mind and
body that the day's work is over and you are free to relax and sleep."*
—*Dr. Andrew Weil*

I believe that the world would be a better place if everyone relaxed in warm
water more often. The only thing better than bathing for relaxation is meditating in the bath. This practice requires a quick, simple setup. Draw yourself a
hot bath in your favorite tub and get in. Feel free to use anything you typically
like with a bath, such as bubbles, salts, candles, or relaxing music. The intention
of this meditation is to focus on the sensation of your body in water. Combined
with the soothing nature of warm water, the practice is especially relaxing.

1. Find a comfortable position in the bath. It might be best to support your head and neck with a towel or pillow (just be sure you won't fall asleep).

2. Check in with your breath. Follow the natural pattern of your inhales and exhales. Notice any sensations of the breath from being in warm water, such as scents or the feeling of steam in your nostrils.

3. Beginning at the tips of your toes and working your way up to the very top of your head, bring your awareness to each inch of your body. You can wiggle your toes and gently flex your feet. Slightly move your ankles, your calves, and your shins.

4. Continue up your entire body, paying attention to the sensation in each little part.

5. Can you feel the slightest pressure of the warm water against every cell in your skin?

6. Give your entire awareness to the sensation of being warm, comfortable, and relaxed while submerged in the water. Come back to your breath whenever your mind starts to wander.

7. When thoughts do arise, notice them, observe them, accept them, and let them go. Return to your breath and the sensation of being in water.

20

TOP OF THE WORLD *10 MINUTES*

We spend so much time hunched over our desks and devices, zooming in, looking at screens and materials that are right in front of us, focusing only on the most urgent thing on our mind, that we often lose the larger perspective. Physically, we can address this problem by straightening up, looking around, and taking a big belly breath in and out. But we also need a solution for our minds. The intention of this practice is to help you untangle from your thoughts and see the big picture again. A note: I prefer this meditation as an indoor meditation. If you are outside, other meditations in this book, such as A Walk in the Woods (page 96) and Chimes (page 94), can help you tune into the nature around you.

1. Find a comfortable seated position. You can sit cross-legged on a cushion on the floor or in a chair. Sit up straight, but don't force perfect posture.

2. Establish a nice easy rhythm with your breath, feeling the full inhale and full exhale, without pushing or pulling.

3. Begin to lengthen the exhale slightly so that it's a bit longer than the inhale.

4. Imagine that you're standing on a mountaintop. You can see for miles in every direction. You're on a path, looking down toward another mountaintop. Take in the views around you. The sky is clear blue, with only a few wispy clouds. There is a gentle breeze. Feel it on your skin. The air smells fresh and clean. The sun is halfway up in the sky, shining and warm, but not too hot.

5. Imagine turning to your right, looking down into the valley at a small lake surrounded by trees. Look across the valley to smaller mountains and hills far off in the distance.

6. Look to your left. Perhaps the slope is steeper on that side. From where you stand, you can see a big river flowing through a deep gorge. The sun

is shining through water vapor that is rising from a waterfall. You see a couple of large birds with brown backs soaring below you.

7. Imagine turning around and looking at the rounded expanse of the mountain. Notice how the sound of the wind changed when you turned.

8. Turn back to the path and look down at your feet. Notice the mix of small pebbles and stones and small green plants and lichen on the path below you.

9. For the next 5 minutes, make your way along the path to the other peak. Be conscious of your footsteps landing on the terrain. Observe the best placement of your feet as you encounter small rocks and roots. Every few steps, take a moment to look around as you did before. How has the light shifted? What can you see now that you couldn't see before? Has the wind picked up?

10. Continue along the path until you reach the other peak. Conclude this meditation when you've reached the other peak, or whenever you are ready. Return your attention to your breath, following each inhale and exhale. As you slowly open your eyes, notice the sounds and smells and sensations that surround you. Note the freshness of the present moment and how your mind is completely clear, calm, and open.

TIP: Reading these instructions *while* doing the meditation can diminish the complete experience, so the best approach is to read them several times and internalize them and then guide yourself through them. The idea is to really take your time, to feel all of the sensations, to hear the birds and feel the breeze, and to stop and look around every few steps.

PART II
Release Stress

As we go through our day-to-day lives, we naturally accumulate stress and tension, which manifests as exhaustion, lack of focus, resentments toward others, and sometimes even physical aches and pains. The meditations in this section are designed to help you mitigate this daily dose of stress by taking the time to completely release it. They can all be done in the morning, during the day as a quick reset, or at the end of the day, when you're back home and transitioning into downtime.

FULL OF LIGHT 5 TO 10 MINUTES

The concept of light is often associated with truth, wisdom, and insight. There are countless depictions of light emanating from spiritual figures across religions. Popular sayings like "shine a light on it" reflect the theme of light representing illumination or clarity. In this meditation, you will visualize yourself as a light source radiating light from the core of your abdomen, through your entire body, and out into the external world. After this meditation, you'll be able to resume your day with renewed clarity and peace.

1. Find a comfortable seated position. You can sit cross-legged on a cushion on the floor or in a chair. Sit up straight, but don't force perfect posture.

2. Gently close your eyes.

3. Inhale through your nose and exhale completely, letting out a big sigh through your mouth. Repeat 3 times, deepening the breath each time.

4. Relax your body and release all thoughts from your mind.

5. Return to a natural breathing pattern and bring your attention to the feeling of the breath in your belly. Pay attention to the gentle expansion when you inhale and the relaxation when you exhale. Begin to breathe more deeply, perhaps with a count of 5 on the inhale and a count of 10 on the exhale.

6. Stay with the breath, focusing on the sensation it produces in your belly.

7. In the center of that sensation, identify a feeling of warmth. As you focus on the warmth in your belly, imagine it is glowing faintly.

8. With each inhale, visualize the warmth growing in intensity and size, and with each exhale, visualize the glow becoming a little brighter and larger.

9. Repeat this pattern for the next 15 to 20 breaths, visualizing the warm light slowly filling your entire torso, your legs, your shoulders, your arms, and your head.

10. When your entire body is filled with the warm light, feel it move out through the skin of your chest, your back, your arms, hands, and feet until your entire body is warm and glowing inside and out.

11. Imagine that you are alone in a dark room and that the warm glow of your body casts a gentle light all around.

12. As thoughts arise, acknowledge them, and let them go.

13. Return to your breath, to the rhythmic count of 5 on the inhale and 10 on the exhale, and to the glowing warmth you have become.

14. When the meditation feels complete, slowly move your fingers, then your toes. Stretch your arms out wide to the sides, then up overhead. Rest your arms at your side. Take a deep slow inhale through your nose and release it all through your mouth.

15. Get up slowly. See if you can retain the feeling of warm, calm confidence in your core throughout your day.

TIP: This meditation can be easier if you're warm, but it can also help warm you up if you're cold.

EYE OF THE STORM 10 TO 15 MINUTES

As a teenager I experienced a horrible headache that I've never forgotten. It would not go away no matter what I did. Finally, I gave up and got in bed. I tried to focus my attention on something else, but the pain was too acute. I tried to "will it" away, but that didn't work either. In desperation, I decided to become curious. What was it inside my head that could cause so much pain? Why was it there? I decided to do the opposite of what I had been doing: I focused directly on the pain, seeking to pinpoint the exact location of its source and giving my complete awareness over to the sensation. As I got closer and closer to the pain, I realized that there was movement to it and—to my surprise— space within it. It was as if there was an eye of the storm inside the pain, where the sensation wasn't as sharp. I noticed that by focusing on the center of the pain, breathing slowly, and giving my attention to calming my aggravated nerves, I could feel it diminishing. A little while later, the pain was gone. Yogis I have spoken with have shared similar experiences with me. I've found this technique helpful with various types of aches and pains throughout my life. If pain is a source of stress for you, give this meditation a try.

1. Lie on your back on a firm, comfortable surface, such as a yoga mat or carpet.

2. Take a slow, deep inhale through your nose. Release it all on the exhale with a sigh through your mouth. Repeat this 5 times, each time lengthening the inhale and the exhale.

3. Soften your gaze or gently close your eyes.

4. When we have pain in one area of our body, we often get tense in other parts of our body. Scan your body to notice any areas of stress or tension. Make an effort to completely relax your entire body.

5. Relax your face. Relax your jaw muscles. Relax your tongue.

6. Establish a rhythm with your breath, breathing in on a count of 5 or 6 and breathing out on a count of 10 or 12. Find a rhythm that works for you. This rhythm should be comfortable and relaxing and not make you feel like you're gasping for air.

7. Now, identify the area of pain in your body. Find the specific place, the epicenter of the pain. Focus on that place while maintaining your breath and keeping your entire body still and relaxed.

8. As you zoom in on the sensation, pay attention to what you notice about this specific pain. Don't label or describe it in your mind. Just get curious about it. What does it feel like?

9. As you continue to maintain a steady breathing rhythm, see if you can relax the area of your body that's hurting. Focus on calming that small cluster of nerves. Perhaps you notice that there is a space within the pain where there is no sensation. If so, envision soothing the aggravated nerves from within. You're comforting that area, giving it gentle attention. Stay with this focus for several minutes. Imagine that you're releasing the pain with each exhale and bringing in calm relaxation with each inhale.

10. When you feel ready, bring your attention back to your whole body. Scan it from head to toe. Notice how completely relaxed you feel, how your perception of the pain has diminished. Wiggle your fingers and toes. Stretch your arms out wide and up overhead. Take a deep breath, open your eyes, and get up slowly.

NOTE: This meditation should not be done in lieu of proper medical attention and care. Any acute or chronic pain should be addressed with your doctor.

SUPER THOUGHTS 10 TO 15 MINUTES

Not all thoughts are created equal. In this meditation, you will focus on a thought that is helpful and positive. Unlike meditations in which you focus intently on a specific phrase, in this meditation you will focus on an entire thought, holding awareness of all aspects and facets of that thought. As an example, I had a recent experience with my wife and young daughter. We were playing together in the living room. I was completely immersed in the moment, but for a split second I had a moment of profound awareness. In words, the thought was *This is my life*, but in my mind and body, it manifested as a complex sense of gratitude, pride, responsibility, and humility. Because of that experience, it is now a thought that I can re-create and enter into whenever I want. You may have a thought like that from recent memory, or you can create one based on your relationships, career, or experiences. It should be profound, positive, and real—wholly consistent with your understanding of yourself.

1. Find a comfortable seated position. You can sit cross-legged on a cushion on the floor or in a chair. Sit up straight, but don't force perfect posture.

2. Inhale deeply and on the exhale, let out all of the air with a big sigh through your mouth. Repeat 3 times.

3. Gently close your eyes.

4. Scan your body and relax any spots that feel tense.

5. Breathing naturally, bring your awareness to the entirety of each inhale and exhale.

6. Allow any lingering thoughts to drift away.

7. Bring to mind the thought that you've selected for this practice. Place that thought in the center of your attention. Let it occupy your mind and allow space for all associated imagery and emotions that accompany it.

8. Now imagine the thought as an object. Perhaps it is the only object in a sunlit room. Try to move around it, looking at it from one side, then from the other. Look at it from above and from below.

9. Without judging or labeling anything, notice the shape of the thought, its color, and its texture.

10. Observe the complexity and scale of this thought.

11. As powerful and important as this thought is to you, remember that it is merely a thought, a creation of your mind.

12. Stay with this exercise for the next 10 to 15 minutes. When the meditation feels complete, let the thought dissolve, leaving you with a clear mind.

13. Come back to your breath. Feel your body in space. Open your eyes. As you return to your day, notice whether you are more sensitive to the thoughts that rise up in your mind and whether you can view them as impermanent objects that come and go.

TWO INCHES TALLER

We all spend too much time hunched over our computers and phones. This poor posture can have serious consequences, diminishing blood flow to our brains, putting unnatural tension on our necks, and reducing our lung capacity. Research shows that good posture positively affects our self-confidence and how other people perceive us. Plus, it simply feels good to sit or stand up straight and tall. In this meditation, you'll turn your awareness to maintaining an optimal posture for the amount of time you've allocated. This meditation is great to do while walking, but you can be seated if you prefer. If anything about this meditation produces sharp pain, do not do it, and make an appointment to speak with your physician.

1. Begin by checking your lower back. There should be a nice, comfortable curve in your lower spine. To find the position, play with tilting your pelvis forward, then backward. Seek the position where you feel a slight engagement of your abdominal muscles and equally slight engagement of your lower back muscles. Neither muscle group should be gripping tightly, but both should be activated.

2. Lengthen your spine up through the top of your head, reaching the crown of your head toward the sky. Lengthen your neck.

3. Pull your shoulder blades together, then relax them and let them set naturally into a comfortable position down your back.

4. Lift your shoulders up toward your ears, then let them drop to a comfortable position. Make sure that your ears are positioned over your shoulders.

5. Without changing anything in your lower back or neck, gently lift your chest.

6. Relax your jaw and all of the muscles in your face.

7. Take a big inhale and let out all the air with a big sigh through your mouth. Repeat.

8. Check that all the muscles in your body are completely relaxed except those enabling you to maintain your posture. Those should be gently engaged, not tense.

9. For the next 10 to 20 minutes, maintain your posture. Keep your awareness on your body. Do certain areas begin to fatigue more than others? Is this posture comfortable for you? Where does your body feel open, and where does it feel tight?

10. Pay attention to the openness in your lungs and abdomen. Gently relax any areas of the body that feel tense.

11. Return to your breath frequently and maintain a passive awareness. Your body will be sending you a lot of signals. Acknowledge them as they arise, and then let them go.

12. After completing this meditation, notice whether you've become more aware of your posture and whether you carry that awareness throughout the day. You may find that you walk, stand, and sit taller.

TIP: Simply maintaining a strong upright posture can be more work than we realize. As fatigue sets in, your mind will look for ways to make you more comfortable by distracting you with other thoughts. You may also have negative thoughts that accompany fatigue or tension. Remember that a strong upright posture is a positive and natural position for your body. Discomfort is a sign that your body is simply not accustomed to sustaining a good posture.

TRY THIS: Try to avoid "locking" into a rigid perfect posture. Keep your body loose, fluid, and malleable. Play with making tiny adjustments and notice how even the slightest shifts can affect how the posture feels.

ALTERNATE REALITY 10 TO 15 MINUTES

> *"You are what you are and where you are because of what has gone into your mind. You can change what you are and where you are by changing what goes into your mind."*
>
> *—Zig Ziglar*

If I were to ask you to name one or two things about your life that you wish were different, I bet you could name them quickly. In fact, you could probably name 100 things. Seeking, yearning, wishing, and wanting are fundamental aspects of our human nature. The truth is that there's an alternate reality available to you now, free of wanting, wishing, or striving. It is universally applicable to everything in your life. It is real, it is profound, and it holds a more fulfilling life for you within it. When we talk or think about our reality, and especially the things we wish were different, we tend to overlook the degree to which our perceptions of reality are constructed by our minds. If we change our minds, we can literally change our reality. In this practice, you will pick one thing about your life that you wish were different. Then, rather than thinking about how you want it to be different, you're going to identify and focus on what you appreciate about it in its current form. You'll stay in the appreciation mind-set throughout this meditation.

1. Find a comfortable seated position. You can sit cross-legged on a cushion on the floor or in a chair. Sit up straight, but don't force perfect posture.

2. Gently close your eyes.

3. Without changing or controlling your breath, bring your attention to it. Find a place where you feel a pleasant sensation associated with the

breath. It might be the tip of your nose or the top of your lungs, or it might arise in the rise and fall of your abdomen. Focus your attention there for 5 inhales and exhales.

4. Bring to mind an aspect of your life that you wish were different. (For example, *I wish I had more money.*) Don't overthink it. The first thing that comes to mind is often the best thing to work with here.

5. Consider the reasons that you have this wish. If this wish were to come true, what would change? How do you think your relationship with yourself or with others would be better? Drilling down, what is the core driver of this desire? Pause there.

6. Now, look at your current situation and focus on a positive aspect of it. If, for example, you wish you had more money, you might now say, *I like how my current situation forces me to not be wasteful.*

7. For the next several minutes, keep your focus on this area of appreciation.

8. Notice how simply changing the focal point to an area of appreciation begins to shift your perception of your situation. Rather than a problem to fix, it becomes a gift of the here and now. As your perception shifts, you begin to occupy a different mind-set, an alternate reality.

9. Notice the images and emotions that accompany this new reality. Maintain focus on your appreciation for this circumstance.

10. When the meditation feels complete, bring your attention back to your breath. As you go about your day, see if you carry a different perspective on this thing you wished to change. Consider other areas of your life in which you may be wishing for change. Why carry a desire for things to be different when you can feel deep appreciation for how they are?

CHILD'S POSE 5 MINUTES

For this meditation, you will rest in the yoga position called Child's Pose. This pose is restorative, but it involves some active elements and alignment of the body. Be sure to carefully assume the pose before beginning your meditation. Child's Pose offers a great stretch through the back, glutes, and shins. It also places your forehead on the floor, which is a grounding, humbling, and restful position. In this exercise, you will stay with the breath while maintaining an awareness of the sensations created by the pose. If you're unfamiliar with this pose, see the resources section for a link to a demonstration (page 144). Make any adjustments that you need throughout this meditation to stay comfortable.

1. On a yoga mat or comfortable rug on the floor, enter into Child's Pose. Find a version of the pose in which you are completely comfortable and relaxed, one in which nothing feels pinched or uncomfortable.

2. Inhale deeply and let out all the air with a big sigh through the mouth. Repeat 5 times.

3. Soften your gaze or gently close your eyes.

4. Begin inhaling on a count of 5 and exhaling on a count of 10. Keeping the exhale twice as long as the inhale, find the rhythm that is best for you. It may be an inhale of 3 and exhale of 6, or an inhale of 8 and an exhale of 18. Try to exhale completely with each breath. Keep the breath cycle consistent and controlled.

5. Reach your hands out in front of you and then off to one side and then the other. Spend a few breaths in each position, feeling the stretch in your back.

6. Return your hands to a comfortable resting position and stay there for another few minutes.

7. With the coming and going of each breath, become aware of the sensations in your body. Without judgment, without any goal or intended outcome, simply observe the signals your body is sending.

8. As any thoughts arise, acknowledge them and let them go.

9. When your practice is complete, press yourself up gently with your hands, then roll around to a seated position or lie on your back for 1 to 2 minutes. Stand up slowly.

FOUND SOUND 5 TO 10 MINUTES

The renowned yoga and mindfulness teacher Leslie Kaminoff tells the story of a recycling truck emptying a dumpster full of glass bottles outside his window during his morning meditation. The noise was so loud, so disruptive, that his immediate reaction was to be angry. But after many days of hearing the dumpster emptying, he had an epiphany: "Sound" is what is happening outside of us; "noise" is our own interpretation based on our perspective, beliefs, and personal context. We tend to forget that we can choose to react differently. In this practice, you'll identify a sound in your environment. It can be any sound, but it should be something that you don't usually pay attention to or something that you find mildly annoying. The intention here is to give your full awareness to the sound, identifying your internal reaction to that sound, and trying to find some space between the sound and the way in which its "noise" impacts you.

1. Find a comfortable seated position. You can sit cross-legged on a cushion on the floor or in a chair. Sit up straight, but don't force perfect posture.

2. Close your eyes.

3. Take several deep breaths.

4. Allowing your breath to return to its natural rhythm, bring your full awareness to the flow and feeling of each inhale and exhale.

5. Turn your attention to the sounds coming into your ears. What do you hear? Is there a low-level background sound of some machine—perhaps a fan or a furnace? Identify a sound that, if you had a choice, you would change or turn off. What is it about that sound you don't like? Is it the volume? Is it the tone, the texture, or the pitch?

6. Over the next few minutes, stay focused on this particular sound. Consider what is making the sound. Imagine the actual pieces, parts, or anatomical features that, through friction, are creating the sound waves that are traveling to your ears. Consider the path that the sound waves are traveling to get to you.

7. Realize that this sound, like all other sounds you hear, is simply a pattern of energy, disrupting the air in precise vibrations to be created exactly as you hear it. Consider that your brain is designed to identify sounds and give them meaning and that the meaning is subjective. What sounds lovely to some people will grate on others.

8. Try to shift your perspective on this sound. For example, if the sound of the heater fan is bothersome, imagine that you are hearing the fan after days of it being broken.

9. Once you make this shift, try to recognize a distinct space between the "sound" and your perception of "noise." Realize that because you can change your perception, being annoyed by a sound is a *choice*.

10. When the meditation feels complete, come back to your breath. Try to carry this practice of "space" throughout your day. You may notice that you aren't as easily affected by things outside of your control: They are simply happening. There is nothing you can do about them except adjust your perspective and accept the moment for what it is.

SMILE LIKE YOUR LIFE DEPENDS ON IT 5 MINUTES

"The muscles used to make a smile actually send a biochemical message to our nervous system that it is safe to relax the flight, fight or freeze response."

—*Tara Brach*

We normally smile because of how something makes us feel. A smile is an external expression of an internal emotion. But is it possible to *create* happiness or a sense of relaxation just by smiling? In my experience, it is absolutely possible. This meditation is great for turning around the heavy feeling of having a bad day, shedding hard-to-shake stress, or preparing for an important meeting, moment, or interaction.

1. Find a comfortable seated position, ideally somewhere where you won't feel self-conscious about anyone seeing you.

2. Soften your gaze or gently close your eyes.

3. Bring your attention to your breath, following each exhale and inhale for several complete cycles.

4. Pay attention to the sensation of the breath, identifying a particular place in your body—in your nostrils, at the back of your ribs, under your sternum—where the sensation feels pleasant. Focus on that sensation.

5. Gently begin to smile. Smile broadly, but without force. Do not create tension in your facial muscles. Smile as you would naturally, without even trying.

6. As thoughts arise, notice them, accept them, and let them go. Your brain might try to distract you by saying things like *This is weird. What am I doing?* Or your brain might match your smile by offering a funny or happy thought, or it might protest by saying something like *This is fake, I'm actually not happy. I'm upset about....* Whatever your brain does, notice it and then let it pass.

7. Maintain a steady, comfortable rhythm with your breath and maintain a steady, gentle smile for the next few minutes.

8. As you conclude this practice and reenter your daily routine, notice whether you smile more quickly or more broadly. Notice whether you feel a little happier, a little lighter, or more confident.

A TINY WALK 15 MINUTES

When I was a kid growing up in the country, I used to sit and watch ants building their nests. As I watched them carrying materials and food, walking in perfect lines, I was fascinated by how such a complex society could exist in such a tiny physical space. I could stand up, take a few steps, and be in what would seem like a different world to those ants. Like the ants, our day-to-day experience in the world is closely aligned with our human-size houses and cars and roads and toys. Almost everything we interact with and think about is a creation or by-product of our engineered world. Taking time to focus on something that is much smaller than us, to occupy that space and immerse ourselves in that level of scale, affords us an opportunity to totally shift our perspective. In this practice, you'll use a visual focal point to cultivate awareness of the present moment and retune your sensitivity to the world around you.

1. Find a comfortable place to sit or lie down outside, preferably near a tree or a large rock. Be close enough to see the details and textures of the surface, but far enough away to be able to see most of the object.

2. Become aware of your breath. Without changing or controlling your breath cycle, follow it several times. Find a sensation in your breathing on which to focus. This sensation might be in your nostrils, at the back of your throat, or in the rising and falling of your abdomen or chest. Bring your attention there.

3. Imagine that you're watching a tiny insect, as small as the smallest ant you've ever seen, walking up or across the object. It is not particularly fast, but it isn't the slowest insect either. It moves steadily but cautiously, stopping periodically to check the air and wiggle its antennae.

4. Keep your eyes trained on this imaginary creature as it slowly climbs. Notice how it needs to carefully navigate the textured surface on which it's walking. Its little feet need to find purchase with each step.

5. Don't rush and don't skip ahead. The creature you're envisioning can only climb as fast as it climbs: slowly, steadily.

6. For the next several minutes, keep your eyes focused on the path of this insect.

7. As thoughts interrupt, acknowledge them, perhaps make note of them, but let them go.

8. Return to your breath whenever this happens. Close your eyes for a moment if you need to reset your visual focus.

9. Focus on this creature for the next 5 to 10 minutes, paying close attention to each tiny step it must make.

10. When the practice feels complete, close your eyes and take several deep breaths. Move your body and gently stretch your neck from side to side.

11. As you transition back into your day, notice whether your eyes are steadier. Notice whether this sense of calm focus carries into your thinking and how you speak.

TIP: This meditation may initially feel tedious or tiring. Typically, as our eyes scan our visual world, our minds are accustomed to making quick associations and judgments. It is unusual to tell your eyes where to look and what to see for a prolonged period of time. As a result, this meditation can be challenging, but keep trying it.

10

FRENEMY 5 MINUTES

Much of the stress and anxiety we experience is related to our interactions with other people. As human beings, we crave love, appreciation, and respect. When interactions leave us feeling unloved, unappreciated, or disrespected, we point to the shortcomings of others or seek to diminish the value of their opinions as a way to make ourselves feel better. Though it can be challenging, I can usually identify at least one thing I truly respect about everyone. In this meditation, you're going to identify a person with whom you have frustrations or disagreements or who doesn't seem to like or appreciate you, and you're going to focus on one thing about that person that you admire. This practice will help you reduce, even eliminate, stress or anxiety that you feel as a result of challenging relationships with others.

1. Find a comfortable seated position on a cushion on the floor or in a chair. You can also do this meditation while walking.

2. Establish a straight spine, being mindful of good posture, but don't create any rigid tension in your body.

3. Take a gentle inhale, then exhale completely, letting go of all thoughts and releasing any tension. Repeat.

4. Bring to mind the thing about this person that you admire. Why do you admire this characteristic? Is it unique to this person? Why do you view it as valuable?

5. Over the next several minutes, hold in mind this sense of admiration. How does it make you feel? What thoughts accompany this feeling? How does focusing on this positive attribute shift your overall perception of this person?

6. You aren't trying to actively think of anything, force a feeling, or even answer these questions in a direct way. Rather, you're offering this prompt to your mind and observing, passively, without judgment or attachment, the thoughts and emotions that follow.

7. After you've completed this meditation, notice whether your interactions with this person start to feel different. By becoming more attuned to a mind-set of appreciation and admiration, your communications with the person may improve.

GETTING REAL

As humans, we are easily distracted by what's bright and shiny—new people, new material things, or interesting opportunities. Social media companies and online retailers craftily exploit this weakness every day. We are constantly bombarded with hundreds of advertising messages and images, many of which catch our attention and lure us to click. The chatter of our internal minds has a similar grip on us, yanking us in different directions, telling us what to do and what to think about. Just as the perfectly filtered messages online appear truer than they actually are, so do our thoughts and experiences. In this meditation, you will look past the superficial layers of the world and explore the core substance by asking the simple yet profound question *What is real?*.

1. Find a comfortable seated position. You can sit cross-legged on a cushion on the floor or in a chair. Sit up straight, but don't force perfect posture.

2. Soften your gaze or close your eyes.

3. Take 7 deep breaths. On each exhale, release tension from your body, starting with your head and working your way down to your feet and toes. You are totally calm and completely awake.

4. Allow your breath to return to a natural rhythm.

5. For the next several minutes, maintain an awareness of your breath.

6. In your mind, ask yourself the question *What is real?* You are not seeking definitive answers or insights. You're simply asking the question.

7. As you stay with this question, your brain will want to propose some answers. Acknowledge these answers but let them pass. Then notice your breathing. Is that real? Notice the sensations in your body. Are they real? Again, you are not trying to actually answer the question. You are simply asking it and being receptive to all that occurs in each moment spent with it.

8. Although it may seem strange to pose a question without forming an answer, you're actually shifting your relationship with your brain from one in which all thoughts trigger actions, emotions, or more thoughts to one in which you remain in the moment.

9. If thoughts, emotions, or external distractions arise, acknowledge them and let them go without judgment or attachment. Return to the question *What is real?*

10. As you continue about your day, allow this question to serve as an instantaneous cue, a tiny meditation that brings you back into the present moment whenever your analytical mind tries to take over.

12

GIVE IT AWAY 5 TO 10 MINUTES

Simple acts of generosity can have as much positive impact on the giver as the receiver. Yet many of us spend most of our time and energy trying to "get" and very little trying to "give." In this meditation, you'll focus on the concept of generosity. How can you be more generous with your time, your attention, your material possessions, and your money and with your words, thoughts, and actions as they relate to other people? How can you be more generous with yourself? You can approach this meditation as a reflective internal meditation or as a writing meditation. The objective is to stay close to the mind-set of generosity.

1. Begin by finding a comfortable seated position. You can sit cross-legged on a cushion on the floor or in a chair. If you are planning to do a writing meditation, have a pen and some paper near you.

2. Soften your gaze or gently close your eyes.

3. Take a deep slow inhale through your nose, and let out all the air with a big sigh through your mouth. Repeat 3 times.

4. Allow your breath to return to its natural rhythm and bring your awareness to the flow of each inhale and exhale. Release any lingering thoughts from your mind.

5. Allow the concept of generosity to fill your mind and body. What is generosity? Where does it come from? How does it feel to be generous? How have you been generous in your life? Watch what arises in your mind.

6. Become curious about what comes up for you. Begin identifying ways you'd like to be more generous, and take note of areas of your life in which you are already quite generous. Rather than judging yourself or the generosity of others, remain curious about what generosity is and how it feels. If you are writing, let the words flow freely.

7. Stay with this exploration of generosity. Avoid gripping onto any one notion or seeking any clear answers. Simply explore. Allow thoughts to arise, acknowledge them, and let them go.

8. If you find your mind wandering, come back to your breath and focus on the simple idea of generosity. Consider the generosity implicit in breathing—in the release of oxygen by plants and in the use of that oxygen by your cells to keep everything running.

9. Consider generosity part of the cycle of passing energy and resources from one being to another. Reflect on this generosity on both a small and a large scale.

10. Remember that meditation is an act of generosity to yourself.

TIP: After you complete this meditation, try bringing more generosity into your life. Sign up to volunteer, donate to charity, or share relevant knowledge or skills with people who need them. Give of your time, energy, money, or things with no expectations and without caveats. You'll feel great.

EXPERT IN BEING YOU 10 MINUTES

Have you ever stopped to consider that there is no one else in the world who knows you as well as you do? We are so often overcome by regrets or hopes or the ways we want to change that we don't give ourselves enough credit for how much we know about ourselves right now. Meditation affords you the opportunity to deepen your self-knowledge. Chances are that you already know more about yourself than you realize. In this meditation, hold in mind the confidence that you know yourself better than anyone else and the power that confidence gives you in building the life you want and deserve.

1. Find a comfortable seated position. You can sit cross-legged on a cushion on the floor or in a chair. Sit up straight, but don't force perfect posture.

2. Soften your gaze or gently close your eyes.

3. Take several deep breaths.

4. Allow your breathing to return to its natural rhythm and bring your attention to a specific place where you feel the sensation of your breath.

5. In your head or softly out loud, repeat the following phrases: *I know myself. I am an expert in me. What does it mean to know myself?*

6. Over the next several minutes—without seeking insight, searching for specific answers, or defining what comes to mind—give your attention to the feeling of knowing and understanding yourself on the deepest level.

7. Notice any thoughts that try to disrupt your focus or make you doubt your knowledge of self. Remember that you do know yourself—better than anyone else. Remember that meditation is a way to deepen this understanding.

14

DON'T KEEP GOING 5 MINUTES

The ability to face adversity is a valuable life skill, as is committing to seeing things to their conclusion. But feeling wrought with stress and anxiety through the process is neither necessary nor healthy. Meditation encourages us to pause this "keep going" attitude in order to find some calm and relief from the daily grind. In this meditation you will explore the space between doing and pausing. For many of us, our ambition causes stress. But it doesn't have to be that way.

1. Find a comfortable seated position. You can sit cross-legged on a cushion on the floor or in a chair. Sit up straight, but don't force perfect posture. This practice also works well as a walking meditation.

2. Soften your gaze or gently close your eyes.

3. Without changing or controlling your breath, bring your attention to it. Identify a specific sensation, perhaps at the tip of your nose, roof of your mouth, top of your chest, or back of your sternum, where the breath feels pleasant.

4. In your head or softly out loud, repeat the following phrases: *I am capable. I am calm. I am confident. I am relaxed.*

5. For the next 5 minutes, continue to slowly repeat these phrases.

6. If you find your mind is wandering, pause and return to your breath.

7. Keep your focus on these phrases, staying completely present with the rhythm and meaning of your words.

8. The purpose of this meditation, like all meditations, is to cultivate an awareness of the present moment. Stay in the moment—free from striving, free from grit. Remain present. Observe how the meaning of the words affects your emotional state.

FORGIVENESS 10 TO 20 MINUTES

Much of the stress and anxiety we carry is related to our relationships with other people and our relationship with ourselves, particularly around events and experiences that happened in the past. Given that the past is the past, and there is nothing that can change it, forgiveness is a powerful and underutilized tool for living a more fulfilled life in the present moment. In this practice, you are going to grant yourself—and those who have let you down in the past—complete and total forgiveness, without conditions or expectations.

1. Find a comfortable seated position. You can sit cross-legged on a cushion on the floor or in a chair. Sit up straight, but don't force perfect posture.

2. Extend upward through the top of your head.

3. Soften your gaze or gently close your eyes.

4. Take a slow, deep breath in through your nose and let it all out through your mouth with an "ahhh" sound. Repeat 4 times. Think about lengthening your spine on each inhale and releasing all tension from the body on each exhale.

5. Allow your mind to be clear: absent of worry, free of thoughts.

6. Let your breath return to a natural rhythm and follow each inhale and exhale for several breaths. You can return to this point at any time in the practice.

7. Begin to explore the feeling of forgiveness. Forgive yourself for the mistakes that nag you. Forgive yourself for letting them nag you. Forgive anyone in your life for whom you harbor resentment, disappointment, or anger. In your mind and body, experience the sensation of total, unconditional forgiveness.

8. What does it feel like to completely forgive? Does the negativity, the stress, the resentment, or the tightness start to diminish? Do they dissolve completely?

9. From a mind-set of forgiveness, see if each breath feels freer and more relaxing.

10. Stay with this feeling of forgiveness. Explore the many people or circumstances you can forgive. Explore the feelings that come with doing so. Do you feel clarity and comfort? Do you feel a twinge of fear, of vulnerability? Is there any resistance to actually letting go of these feelings you've held onto?

11. Through the rest of this meditation, return to your breath when you find your mind start to intrude. Try to stay with the feeling of total forgiveness.

12. See if this feeling stays with you through the rest of your day, or even longer.

WHAT TRULY MATTERS 20 MINUTES

We tend to believe that many things in life are extremely important, and we act accordingly—reacting to this, reacting to that, running through our days tending everything we decide is urgent. In this meditation, you'll explore what happens to your state of mind when you temporarily mute your automatic beliefs, attitudes, and actions around what you think is important. It will help you take a step back and gain perspective on what truly matters.

1. Find a comfortable seated position. You can sit cross-legged on a cushion on the floor or in a chair. This meditation also works well as a walking meditation.

2. Soften your gaze and become aware of your breath.

3. Follow several complete cycles of inhales and exhales.

4. Bring your attention to a specific sensation in your breathing. This sensation will be your anchor for the remainder of this meditation. Return to it whenever you find your mind or body becoming restless.

5. As thoughts, sounds, or sensations arise during this meditation, ask these questions: *Is this true? Is this important?*

6. Resist the temptation to try to answer the questions. In this meditation, simply asking them is enough to begin developing a passive detachment from your thoughts. Some thoughts, sounds, or interruptions may be true and important. Some may be true but not really important, some may be neither true nor important. Our default is to assume that just because we think, hear, see, or feel something, it is both true and important. This meditation will help you cultivate discernment.

7. Stay with this quality of mind through the meditation, maintaining a connection to the breath as your anchor. Carry this mind-set throughout your day and notice how it helps you channel your energy.

17

CHIMES 5 TO 10 MINUTES

The sound of wind chimes has a unique relaxing quality. In this simple meditation, you'll focus on the sound from either real wind chimes (if you have some hanging nearby and it's a windy day) or a recording (you can easily find free recordings online). Like other aural-based meditations in this book, the intention here is to bring your total awareness to the sound of the chimes as it arrives at your ears. You will fully accept the sound while remaining completely aware of the present moment.

1. Find a comfortable seated position. You can sit cross-legged on a cushion on the floor or in a chair. Sit up straight, but don't force perfect posture. Position yourself near wind chimes that you hear clearly. If you're listening to a recording, press play.

2. Take several slow, deep breaths. Let any thoughts drift away.

3. Allow your breath to return to its natural rhythm and bring your focus to a specific sensation within the cycle of your inhales and exhales. It could be the tip of your nose, the back of your throat, or the rise and fall of your rib cage.

4. Turn your attention to the sound of the chimes. Try to immerse yourself in the sound waves of each note. Feel the sound fill your body.

5. Keep your attention on the sound of the chimes for the duration of this meditation.

6. If thoughts, sensations, or other sounds distract from your focus, return to your breath and the sound of the chimes.

A WALK IN THE WOODS 25 MINUTES

The vast majority of human evolution occurred while we lived in a very close relationship to nature. Only within the past 100 years have we begun spending much more time indoors. And in only the past couple of decades have we begun spending most of our time staring at, or living under, artificial lights. Fresh air and the soothing sounds and sights we experience while outdoors are revitalizing on a primal level. In this mindfulness meditation practice, all you need is a peaceful nature trail. If you live in a city, find a path in a park. Try to get away from the sounds and sights of bustling humanity. Just find the most natural environment that you can.

1. Once you're on the path, begin walking at a comfortable, natural pace. The intention of this meditation, like all others, is to cultivate and sustain total awareness of the present moment, so there's no need to rush.

2. Without changing or controlling its natural rhythm, bring your attention to your breath. Observe the easy coming and going of each inhale and exhale. Bring your focus to a specific sensation within the cycle of your breath. It could be the tip of your nose, the back of your throat, or the rise and fall of your rib cage.

3. Allow any thoughts in your head to dissolve away, coming into total awareness of each movement your body makes as you walk—from your fingertips to your shoulders, your neck, your torso and your hips, knees, ankles, and toes.

4. Try to gently improve your posture and deepen your breathing.

5. As you continue on your walk, pay attention to what you're experiencing. How does the ground feel under your feet? What sound do your feet make touching the ground? Can you make your footsteps almost silent without dramatically changing your gait?

6. How does the sound of the wind change as you move along the path? Can you hear birds? Perhaps children playing? Is there moving water?

7. Look up at the sky. What are the clouds doing?

8. You are moving through the world, an observer of all that you see, hear, feel, smell, touch, and experience. You are completely in the present.

9. What does the external world bring up in your internal world? As thoughts arise, acknowledge them, accept them, and let them go. Bring your focus back to your experience in the present moment.

10. When you conclude this meditation and return to your day, notice how you feel. Are you more relaxed? Do you feel refreshed or revitalized? Do you have more clarity? Remember that you can bring the same level of awareness that you brought to your walk to every moment in your day.

FULL OF GRATITUDE 5 MINUTES

Many gurus and mindfulness experts espouse the benefits of a gratitude practice. I personally believe it is one of the best methods for creating near-immediate mental calm. A stark difference from the mental states of analysis, calculation, planning, and worry, a state of gratitude is one of peaceful acceptance. Feeling grateful may be the most simple and elegant shortcut to a calm, clear mind. The best part is you can do this anywhere, anytime, regardless of what's going on in your life. You can *always* find something to be grateful for—if only the air you breathe.

1. Wherever you are and whatever you're doing, find a comfortable position—you can be seated, standing, or lying down. You can be anywhere. Lengthen your spine, lifting through the top of your head.

2. Gently close your eyes or soften your gaze.

3. Bring your attention to your breath. Notice the inhale and exhale without doing anything to change or control it.

4. Clear your mind of all thoughts and worries. Let your thoughts dissolve and your mind become quiet.

5. Now, without focusing on any one particular aspect of your life, think of something that fills you with gratitude. It could be a person, a material thing, a sensation, a smell, or a food. The first thing that comes to mind may surprise you, but stay with it and spend time with it. It could be the color of a tree trunk, or the sound of a person's voice, or the crunch of a potato chip.

6. For the next 5 minutes, allow new ideas of gratitude to arise in your mind. Give each one attention. Spend time with it. Observe the aspects of each idea for which you are particularly grateful. You may find, as I have, that this technique becomes your go-to mindfulness technique. Once you're in a state of gratitude, everything shifts.

TIP: Don't judge the things that come to you in gratitude. Once, while doing this practice, I had an immediate and overwhelming gratitude for turtles, of all things. I still have no idea where that came from, or why it was hanging out in my "gratitude tank," but I spent time with it and identified a whole host of things I like about turtles. And you can bet I've never looked at turtles the same way since. The surprises are fun and worth your gratitude.

VARIATIONS: If you're looking for a little more guidance, you can assign a theme to your gratitude practice, such as:

- People in your family
- Things that are blue
- Things in your home

THE LAUGHING HEART

I find that poetry, with its powerful economy of language, can conjure emotions and insights that aren't as easily accessed through other forms of art. For this practice, you'll want to find a poem that you appreciate. Whether you are into poetry or not, chances are that you can find a poem that draws you in and speaks to you. If you need some help, here are some poets to check out: Shakespeare, Ted Kooser (former U.S. Poet Laureate), Mary Oliver, or Dr. Seuss. There is a poem by Charles Bukowski I particularly appreciate called "The Laughing Heart." Whenever I read it, I find it reassuring, grounding, and inspiring. It's almost become my anthem. Whichever poem you choose, have it in front of you for this meditation (ideally in printed form, because screens can be distracting).

1. Find a comfortable seated position. You can sit cross-legged on a cushion on the floor or in a chair.

2. Sit upright but positioned so you can comfortably read the poem for several minutes.

3. Read the poem slowly. You can read it out loud or in your head. Pay attention to the sound and the shape of each word. Pay attention to the way each word adds depth of meaning to the words that preceded it.

4. As you read, note how your mind and emotions respond. Do certain words or phrases create different responses than others?

5. Can you read the poem and find different meanings if you change the emphasis on certain words?

6. Notice how language affects you. On the page, words are just shapes, made up of light and dark spaces. How we interpret them is based on our learning, cultural conditioning, attitudes, and beliefs. Try looking at the poem without reading it. How does doing so change the experience? How does your brain respond?

7. Just as we have the ability to control the information we consume, we have the ability to shift how the information affects us.

8. For the final 2 minutes of this meditation, close your eyes and return to your breath.

9. Take a moment to reflect. How was your experience with this poem? Did you read it in a way that you hadn't before? Did you discover a new insight? Did you notice any new or unexpected emotions or sensations? Written language is so deeply connected to our experience in the world that we often don't stop to think about it. Remember that what we read, how we read, and the ways reading affects our state of mind are all within our control. We can bring as much awareness to what we're reading, how we're reading it, and how it affects us as we bring to any meditation.

PART III
Drift Off to Sleep

In this section, you will find 20 meditations to help you achieve deep and restful sleep. Several of them are meant to be done directly before your bedtime routine. Others are guided meditations, designed to quiet your mind with calming visualizations, and others will help you find deep relaxation within the comfort of your own bed. All of the practices can be done at any time of day if needed. And if you found that some meditations in the previous sections helped you sleep better, feel free to try them as sleep meditations as well.

PINNACLE

Some people view life as a series of obstacles to be assessed and navigated, some view it as a range of peaks and valleys with inevitable highs and lows, and some view it as an unrelenting slog. Whatever your perspective, consider right now that life is actually none of those narratives, that it is simply the present moment and that your experience of it—whether viewed as good or bad or as part of a larger story—is a creation of your mind. And as you train your mind through meditation, you can fundamentally change how you experience life. For example, another way of looking at life is that you are, right now, living in a peak experience, infinitely rich in fulfillment and harmony. By cultivating an awareness of the present moment, you can exist in a constant state of clarity, acceptance, and equanimity.

1. Find a comfortable seated position. You can sit cross-legged on a cushion on the floor or in a chair. You can also do this meditation while walking.

2. Soften your gaze or gently close your eyes.

3. Bring your attention to your breath, to each inhale and exhale. Identify a sensation in the cycle of your breathing where you feel it the most— perhaps in the roof of your mouth, the bottom of your throat, or just behind your belly button. Keep your focus there.

4. You have arrived. This is the moment that you've been waiting for. You don't need to wait any longer. This moment, right now, is your complete life experience. There is no past. There is no future. There is only now. This is the pinnacle.

5. Take 5 gentle, full, deep breaths.

6. You are here in this moment. Be present with it, with any sounds or sensations, any thoughts that percolate, the coming and going of each breath.

7. You aren't trying to think anything. You aren't trying to be or feel or experience anything specific. You are passively observing, accepting what comes as it comes. If distractions arise, return to your breath. Your entire life experience, your complete reality, is occurring within you and around you right now.

8. When you are ready to conclude this meditation, draw in a deep inhale through your nose, and exhale completely through your open mouth with an "ahhh" sound. Repeat 3 times. Stretch your arms out to your sides, then up overhead.

9. Get up slowly. See if you can carry a sense of calm satisfaction and peaceful fulfillment through your evening routine and as you head off to bed.

BED IN THE FOREST 15 MINUTES

We all like to feel grounded. But as we go through our days, bombarded by thoughts and experiences outside our control, it's easy to drift away from the feelings of stability and security that are available to us. Over time, perpetual rumination, worry, anxiety, and burnout can result. To reconnect with a rooted and stable state of mind, we can turn our attention to one of the most omnipresent forces in our lives: gravity.

1. Lie on your back on a comfortable surface such as a yoga mat, carpet, or bed.

2. Soften your gaze or gently close your eyes.

3. Inhale deeply and slowly through your nose. Let out all the air through your mouth with an "ahhh" sound. Repeat 5 times.

4. Allow your breath to return to its natural rhythm and become aware of the sensations it produces—the gentle rise and fall of your chest and abdomen, the soft flow of air through your nose and throat. Pick a spot where you feel the breath and focus on it.

5. Now imagine that you are in a warm, sunlit forest. The back of your head, shoulders, thighs, calves, and heels are resting in the soil. Feel the warm earth holding you, shaped perfectly around the back of your body.

6. On top of the soil, tucking you in on all sides, is a blanket of leaves. They gently press against you.

7. Around your feet and legs are ferns growing in bunches, gently wrapping your legs.

8. A soft sheet of moss is covering your upper legs and abdomen.

9. Trees are all around you. Looking up, you see their leaves and needles dancing and swaying in the breeze and the soft blue sky above them.

10. You are heavy and rooted, as though you've been here for 10,000 years, and you'll remain here, perfectly still, forever.

11. A beam of sunlight pokes through the branches. You feel the warm light on your face and chest.

12. Lie here for the next 10 minutes, staying with the feelings of warmth, security, stability, and permanence. You are heavy, unmoving, comfortable.

13. If your mind drifts, acknowledge any thoughts that arise, accept them, make note of them, and let them slip away. Return to your breath and your bed in the forest.

WARM FEET, COOL HEAD 5 MINUTES

When we're trying to fall asleep, temperature matters. With heating and cooling systems and tons of options for mattresses, sheets, pillows, and blankets, it's easy to create our ideal sleeping conditions. (If you haven't given your sleeping environment this much attention, you might want to do so.) In this meditation, you will bring your awareness to the temperature of your core and extremities, appreciating all the comfort where it exists and making adjustments anywhere it's lacking.

1. Begin this meditation lying on your back in your bed. Tuck yourself in as you normally do.

2. Gently close your eyes.

3. Draw in a deep, slow inhale through your nose. Exhale completely through your open mouth with an "ahhh" sound.

4. Allow your breath to return to its natural rhythm.

5. Scan your body and note any areas that feel too warm or too cold. Make any adjustment you need within your blankets to get the right temperature. You may feel that certain parts of your body are still too warm or too cold. You may find that part of you is warm and part of you is cold, but that you like it that way.

6. Bring your attention to your ears. Are they warm? Bring your hands up and touch them.

7. Place your hands on your head. Is it warm?

8. Without sitting up, run your hands down your upper body, feeling it from the outside and inside. Notice the exchange of warmth between your hands and your body. Notice the way your body feels on the inside. How do your hands feel?

9. Relax your hands and let them rest at your sides.

10. Take several deep breaths, relaxing completely, and scan your entire body again.

11. You are comfortable and relaxed, just the right temperature. Hold this thought in your mind as you drift off to sleep.

SATELLITE VISION 10 MINUTES

It can be a healthy (if uncomfortable) realization that we're mere specks in a vast universe. While we worry and work and argue and make plans, Earth, hurling through space, occupies a vanishingly small portion of our solar system, which in turn occupies a tiny corner of our galaxy, which in turn occupies an almost negligible area within the known universe. When we take time to recalibrate our sense of scale, we can reconnect with our humility, insignificance, and true sphere of influence. If accepting the smallness of our influence sounds demoralizing, don't worry—it can be deeply empowering. On the grand scale of space and time, we have very little power. But this realization helps us remember the important areas in our lives in which we do have power: our relationship with ourselves and our ability to do good and meaningful work.

1. Find a comfortable seated position. You can sit cross-legged on a cushion on the floor or in a chair or do this meditation lying down. If seated, sit up straight without forcing perfect posture.

2. Soften your gaze or gently close your eyes.

3. Without trying to change or control your breath, bring your attention to it. Notice how it feels, the rise and fall of your chest, the expansion of your abdomen, the flow of air through your nose and throat. Stay with your breath for the next minute or so. See if you can maintain focus on it in each moment.

4. When you are ready, imagine that you are able to see yourself from 3 feet above your head. What do you see? Your whole body or the movement of your gentle breathing, perhaps?

5. Now slowly elevate up and away from where you're sitting. As you lift up, imagine that you first see your roof, then the roofs of the houses next

110   Meditation for Relaxation

door, then all the roofs in the neighborhood. Notice the cars on the streets and the trees and yards. Your roof shrinks from view. As you continue to rise, you can see major highways and factories and airports and lakes and mountain ranges and rivers.

6. Farther up, you can see cities and parts of several states.

7. Soon, you can see entire countries. Zooming up faster now, you see Earth becoming smaller and smaller.

8. You see each of the planets of the solar system, the sun, then the entire solar system. The sun now looks like every other star. Your entire field of vision fills with suns, some of which are arranged in colorful groups.

9. You see giant suns and tiny suns and soon the entire Milky Way galaxy laid out before you, hundreds of billions of stars and planets.

10. Farther up, another galaxy pops into view, then another, and another, and another, and soon the Milky Way is just a tiny speck.

11. Hold this image in your mind and return to your breath. In this moment, the entirety of the universe is present and available within your mind. Take several breaths here and begin to move back toward the Milky Way.

12. Zoom back into the Milky Way, passing the stars and billions of planets you passed on the way out.

13. You can see our sun now, slowly getting a little bit bigger. As you get closer, you can see all the planets of our solar system, then you can see Earth and the moon, then only Earth as it fills your vision.

14. Zoom back in, all the way down to 3 feet above your head.

15. Return to your breath, return to where you are, the room, the sensations and sounds around you.

A CUP OF TEA 15 MINUTES

Part ritual, part aromatherapy, part comforting warmth, making and enjoying a simple cup of tea with intention and awareness can be an exercise in mindfulness. In this practice, you will make a cup of your favorite tea before bed. There are many caffeine-free herbal teas with soporific qualities. I particularly like chamomile, but you can find one you like. Making and enjoying the tea will be your bedtime meditation.

1. Put a tea bag in your favorite mug, and put a kettle of water on to boil.

2. Take a moment to appreciate this mug. Why is it your favorite? Is it the color, the size, the shape, the way it feels in your hand? Perhaps it reminds you of a person or a place? How was this mug made? What is it made out of?

3. Consider the tea bag. What ingredients are inside of it? Where did they come from? Someone developed that unique recipe and ground up the ingredients. Someone engineered the design of the tea bag and the weaving process to make it. The ingredients were poured into the bag, which was then wrapped, boxed, packaged, shipped, and chosen by you.

4. Consider the importance of the tea bag and the mug and the water. You cannot have a cup of tea without one of these elements. Consider how other things in life rely on yet other things to be useful and enjoyable.

5. When the water is ready, slowly pour it into the cup. Notice how the sound of the water hitting the bottom of the mug differs from the sound it makes hitting the tea bag. Notice how the sound of the water changes as it fills the mug.

6. Notice the steam rising off the top of the water in the mug.

7. As the tea steeps, lean over the steam to feel the humid warmth and smell the fragrance. At first the smell might be mild, but as the tea infuses the water, the steam smells more and more like tea.

8. Take several deep breaths there, drawing in slowly and deeply through your nose, exhaling gently and fully through your mouth.

9. Wrap your hands around the mug to feel the heat, making sure not to touch the ceramic if it's too hot.

10. Notice how the steam moves with the slightest shifts in air pressure.

11. When the tea is as strong as you like it, carefully remove the tea bag from the mug. Pay attention to the sensation of the heat as your fingers work close to the hot water. Notice the dexterity and precision of each movement that your hands are capable of making.

12. Move to a comfortable chair or to your bed, bringing the tea with you.

13. When the tea is cool enough to drink, slowly bring it to your lips. Notice how your mouth forms around the lip of the mug, how your mouth prepares for the hot liquid.

14. Has your breathing changed? Are you tensed up in anticipation of the tea being too hot? Relax any areas in the face or body that feel tense.

15. Take a sip. How does it taste? How would you describe the flavors?

16. Stay attuned to each sensation and thought as you enjoy your tea.

17. Notice how vast and nuanced your range of perceptions can be in such a simple activity. Notice how rich, fulfilling, and fascinating life can be when you're totally aware of the present moment. Notice how time can slow down and expand, if you allow it, in the moments we tend to ignore. Allow the memory of the fragrance, the heat of the steam, and the simple pleasure of drinking the warm tea carry you to a calm and restful sleep.

DEEP BELLY BREATHS 10 MINUTES

One of the "eight limbs" of yoga, *pranayama* is the practice of controlling the breath. In Sanskrit, *prana* means "life force" and *ayama* means "extend or draw out." There are numerous pranayama breathing exercises. To the extent that becoming aware of your breath *is* pranayama, most of the meditations in this book use some pranayama principles. Throughout this meditation, we take breath awareness a step further by following a specific and focused breathing technique.

1. Find a comfortable seated position. You can sit on a cushion on the floor or in a chair. Sit up straight, but don't force perfect posture.

2. Imagine that you're lifting up through the top of your head.

3. Soften your gaze or gently close your eyes.

4. Take a long slow inhale through your nose, then exhale completely through your mouth with an "ahhh" sound. Repeat 5 times.

5. Close your mouth and allow your breath to return to normal. Find the place in your abdomen where you feel your breath the most. Focus on breathing into your belly. Stay with this sensation for several breaths.

6. On your next inhale, imagine the spot in your belly is opening up to pull a rush of air down into the bottom of your lungs. You might feel this breath to be very deep and satisfying.

7. On the exhale, feel your abdomen squeeze in and push the air out up through your lungs, your chest, your throat, and your nose.

8. Inhale again from the bottom of your belly.

9. Repeat the same exhale.

10. Each breath should be long and slow, deep and powerful. Don't rush.

11. Stay with this breathing pattern for the rest of this meditation.

12. Maintain your focus on the sensation of each belly breath.

13. If thoughts arise, acknowledge them without judgment and let them go.

14. When the meditation feels complete, allow your breath to return to its natural rhythm. Notice how you feel. Consider how simply breathing with more focus and intention can cause significant shifts in how you feel.

DINNER PARTY

I remember being a kid, lying in bed and listening to the muted banter of my parents and their friends downstairs. At the time, the sounds of the different voices, their varied tones, the ebb and flow of conversation, and occasional outbursts of laughter were reassuring. Now, I like to imagine my daughter is having the same experience as she falls asleep with her parents chatting downstairs. For all of us, regardless of our upbringing or circumstances, knowing our family and our community are close by is deeply important to our sense of identity, belonging, and fulfillment. In this meditation, you will envision a dinner party with your favorite people, scanning the faces and interactions, and absorbing the sounds of conversation and laughter. This bedtime meditation is meant to bring a deep sense of comfort and calm.

1. Lie on your back on the floor or in your bed.

2. Gently close your eyes.

3. Without changing or controlling your breath, bring your attention to it. Follow each inhale and exhale. Identify a sensation in the cycle of your breathing and turn your focus there.

4. Bring to mind a dinner party in a comfortable, familiar setting. The people at the table are your favorite people, the ones who fill you with joy, the people who know you deeply, love you, and trust you.

5. Look at each person. Without trying to script their words, try to feel the meaning of what they're saying. Are they expressing concern, insight, support? Are their bodies leaning in toward the table or leaning out? Are their hands moving? What does their laugh sound like?

6. Continue to move around the table, appreciating the presence of each person. Our memories of people are often complex, carrying varied and conflicting emotions. Take care not to let your emotional memories carry you away from simply accepting the person without judgment or attachment. Be with them in love and compassion, in the joy of sharing time together.

7. When the meditation feels complete, bring your attention back to your breath.

8. Reflect on how lucky you are to have known these people, to have had them (or to still have them) in your life. Let this gratitude for the people in your life and the comfort of being loved fill your body and mind as you drift off to sleep.

TIP: If people you haven't communicated with in a while show up to your dinner party, consider reaching out to them with a phone call or text. *I was doing this meditation, and you were at my table...* could be a good opener to reconnect. Clearly, they are important to you.

FINDING SILENCE

The soundscape of life is rich, varied, and persistent. In almost all settings, unless we're in an isolation tank, some sound usually calls for our attention. Silence, on the other hand, tends to be more elusive. Although the purpose of meditation is to cultivate a detached awareness of all sensations, thoughts, and stimuli in the present moment, the practice of meditation in total silence can be beneficial. In my experience, silence quickly amplifies the cacophony of my thoughts. But by minimizing external distractions, I find that I'm able to settle into a deeper meditation. This technique can be particularly helpful if you're a beginner.

1. For this meditation, you'll want to lie in bed after your bedtime routine so that you won't need to get up again. Ideally, you'll use earplugs or noise-canceling headphones. If you don't have them, try to prevent all sound from reaching your ears using pillows or blankets.

2. Gently close your eyes.

3. Become aware of the natural rhythm of your breath without trying to change or control it. Follow each inhale and exhale completely.

4. Find a place in the cycle of your breathing where you most notice the sensation, perhaps the tip of your nose, the bottom of your rib cage, or the back of your throat. Shift your focus there.

5. As thoughts arise, notice them, acknowledge them, and let them go.

6. Become aware of how all external sound has stopped. Aside from the faint sound of your breathing or possibly your own heartbeat, you can hear nothing. Notice how this relative silence makes you feel. Try to become curious. What is silence? How is it different from your typical experience with sound? Do you find that your thoughts are "louder"? Can you return to your breath, letting all thoughts dissolve and immersing yourself in the silence?

7. Notice how relaxed your body is, how quiet and calm it has become. In our routine lives, even as we fall asleep, our soundscape is so constant, so pervasive, that we don't realize how much it affects us, and how much we rely on it for our sense of connection to the world.

8. When you are ready to complete this meditation, remove whatever you were using to block sound. While taking several slow, deep breaths, notice how much you can hear. Do you hear sounds that you never noticed before? Settle into sleep mode with gratitude for your ability to hear, appreciation for the familiar sounds around you, and a newfound comfort with total silence.

TIP: I'd encourage you not to become dependent on silence for your meditation. Yes, a peaceful environment is helpful, but always needing silence to meditate misses the point of meditation, which is to accept distractions without judgment.

LIGHT AS LIGHT

The incessant rambling of our thoughts, the unknowable and uncontrollable whims of others, the deep-seated ambitions of our acculturation, and the pervasive forces of our own biochemistry can lead to anxiety, doubt, and fantasy. All of these forces, if we're not paying attention, can confuse our true purpose and obscure our view of reality. But we have a choice. Literally and metaphorically, we can turn toward the light. We can seek out the brightness, the clarity, and the truth and forge a path toward more of it. In this meditation, you will use the concept of "light" to help quiet those "dark" thoughts that tend to grow so loud as we try to fall asleep.

1. Find a comfortable seated position. You can sit cross-legged on a cushion on the floor or in a chair. Sit up straight, but don't force perfect posture.

2. Lift upward through the top of your head.

3. Let go of any tension in your body. Completely relax all muscles that aren't holding you up, and find balance between those that are so that no one muscle group seems to be doing all the work. Remain fluid and relaxed.

4. Take 4 deep and satisfying breaths, making the exhales twice as long as the inhales.

5. Relax your eyebrows, your jaw, and your tongue.

6. Tune in to your breath. Notice the sensation it brings, the flow, the natural rhythm, the reliability with which it comes and goes. Find a sensation in the cycle of your breathing where you feel each exhale and inhale the most. It should be a pleasant feeling. Focus on it.

7. Consider the question *What is light?* Hold the question in your mind while focusing on your breath. You aren't seeking an answer. Simply ask the question *What is light?* and see what comes up.

8. Maybe you feel lightness in your body. Maybe you see a warm glow of lightness. Maybe light speeds all around you.

9. You are present with the question, with your breath, and with this moment. Can you get closer to this moment? Can you get closer to the heart of the question? Can you experience more "lightness" within you? What does it feel like?

10. As thoughts arise, acknowledge them, and let them go without judgment. Continue focusing on the idea of light.

11. Letting go of any mental or physical effort, return to your breath. Notice whether it feels lighter, easier, and more fulfilling with each new inhale and exhale. Notice whether you've embodied a new sense of lightness. This sense is something you can tap into anytime. It is always available to you. Bringing this sense of lightness with you to bed (and into your daily life) can be a powerful antidote to the dark forces of discursive thought, stress, and anxiety.

GET COMFORTABLE 10 MINUTES

As anyone who has ever traveled knows, there is nothing like your own bed. There is comfort in the familiar feel of your mattress, sheets, blankets, and pillows and in the familiar smell of your detergent or fabric softener. There is also comfort in your prebed routine, the layout of your bedroom, and even in the smell of your home and the night sounds you've come to know so well. In this meditation, rather than returning from a trip to appreciate the comfort of where you sleep, you're going to simply pay attention to everything that makes your own bed special and comfortable.

1. Lie on your back in your bed with your arms stretched out, palms facing up, and your feet hip-distance apart.

2. Soften your gaze or gently close your eyes.

3. How do you feel? Are you relaxed? Let go of any tension in your face, your jaw, your neck. Let go of any tension you feel in your body.

4. Without trying to change or control your breath, bring your attention to it. Follow each inhale and exhale.

5. Check in with how you feel now. Are you as relaxed as you can possibly be?

6. Take several deep breaths, then return to a normal breath pattern.

7. Bring your focus to the comfort of your bed, the soft support beneath you. Feel the gentle weight of the sheets and blankets on your whole body and the warmth and security they bring you.

8. Check in with the familiar smell of your room.

9. Identify familiar sounds.

10. Without opening your eyes or looking around, picture your surroundings. Perhaps you see the art on the walls, pictures of friends and family, your clothes strewn about, a pet cozied up in the corner—everything creating a calm, relaxing environment around you.

11. Feel the comfort of your pillow beneath your head.

12. Come back to your breath. As thoughts, sounds, or sensations arise, notice them and, without judgment, let them drift away. Return to your breath and the comfort of your own bed.

13. Staying in this feeling of warmth, let go of any lingering effort and allow yourself to drift off to sleep.

FLOATING

Floating on water has a deeply relaxing quality. The sound of the water, the shift in our relationship to gravity, the gentle rocking of waves, the cool (or warm) sensation on our skin. In this meditation, you will imagine that you're floating on your back on a gently rocking body of water. To help facilitate and enhance this meditation, I suggest playing an audio track of water sounds (see resources, page 144).

1. Lie down on your back on a comfortable surface, such as a yoga mat on the floor, a couch, or a bed.

2. Begin playing your audio track.

3. Close your eyes.

4. Take a deep, relaxing breath and allow yourself to fully let go of all thoughts and tensions.

5. Bring your attention to your breath. Don't try to change or control it, simply pay attention to how it feels, to how it moves.

6. Notice the sounds you hear, the sensations, and any thoughts that arise, and return to your breath.

7. In particular, listen to the sounds of the water. What sounds is it making? Do you hear splashing, lapping, rushing? Are there other sounds in the distance? Imagine a blue sky above you, the warm sun, a gentle breeze.

8. Tune in to the experience of floating, of being completely supported by the water below your body. Feel the gentle motion of rocking on the surface of the water. Notice the peacefulness around you and the calm within you.

9. Become completely aware of the present moment. You are awake. You are breathing. You are floating. You are free.

10. As thoughts arise, notice them, acknowledge them, and let them go. Perhaps imagine that they are tiny bubbles rising to the surface of the water around you and gently popping when they reach the air.

11. If you are already in bed, settle into the peace and tranquility you feel and allow sleep to wash over you. If you are not in bed, rise slowly and stay with this feeling of complete relaxation. You can re-create this visualization when it's time to fall asleep.

BIRTHDAY SUIT 15 TO 20 MINUTES

We're accustomed to wearing clothing all the time, and some people feel very uncomfortable being naked. Sure, clothing is important for protection and cultural norms, but it also forms an additional protective layer on which we've come to rely. We have clothes for sleeping, clothes for working, and clothes for playing, and each item of clothing projects something about how we want to present ourselves to the world and how we want others to perceive us. Clothes also constantly touch our skin, the largest organ of our body, so we're in a consistent sensory relationship with them, whether we're conscious of it or not. This meditation helps us reconnect with our truest, purest physical bodies, and it is one you'll want to do in the comfort and privacy of your own home. You may find the sensations on your skin distracting or unnerving and appreciate the sense of putting clothes back on when you're done. Or you may find this exercise liberating and relaxing, in which case you may drift off to sleep without anything on. Don't take this practice too seriously. Have fun with it. Keep your focus on the sensations and the mindfulness practice available to you here.

1. Disrobe completely and get into bed.

2. If lying unclothed in bed is unusual for you, the feeling of the sheets against your skin may be strange in places.

3. As biological creatures, sex and sexuality is core to our existence. Through cultural indoctrination, we may tend to think about nudity as part of sex. In this meditation, try to remove that conditioning from this experience, which is not a sexual one. You are simply wearing no clothes.

4. Take several deep breaths, inhaling slowly through your nose and exhaling completely through your mouth with a gentle "ahhh" sound. Repeat 5 times.

5. Become completely relaxed and allow your breath to return to its natural rhythm.

6. Bring your awareness to your skin. Feel the sensations on every inch of your body. Become aware of any thoughts, insecurities, or worries that arise. Acknowledge them and let them go without judgment.

7. Note the difference between the actual sensations on your skin and the interpretations of those sensations offered by your mind. Let go of what the mind tells you. You are here in your natural state, naked, comfortable.

8. Return to your breath.

TONUS DISSOLVER 10 MINUTES

Tonus is a constant low-level activity in our muscles and tissues, one we rarely notice. When you bring your attention to relaxing a tense muscle, it's easy to release a contraction and bring some ease to the area. But totally and completely relaxing the muscle may require further, deeper concentration. If you are in calm state of mind and follow a simple, focused approach, you can create full-body relaxation on the deepest level. This meditation will guide you through this process—it's a good one to come back to again and again.

1. Lie on your back on a comfortable surface such as a yoga mat or carpet. You can also do this practice in bed before sleep.

2. Place your hands palms up at your sides, just an inch or so away from your hips. Position your feet about hip-width apart with your ankles and toes relaxed.

3. Gently close your eyes.

4. Take 4 deep breaths, inhaling slowly and deeply through your nose, and letting all the air out through your mouth with a gentle "ahhh."

5. Starting at the top of your head, feel the strength of gravity pulling you into deep and total relaxation. Without moving, feel all of your weight being pulled down into the surface beneath you. Feel your skull sinking down, the muscles in your scalp and face relaxing completely with the pull of gravity, and your shoulders, elbows, hips, knees, and ankles sinking deeper and deeper into the earth.

6. Feel your jaw muscles and your tongue release. Feel your lips and all the tiny muscles around your eyes ease.

7. When you have moved through your entire body, check to make sure you haven't introduced tension anywhere at all. You should be completely, entirely, deeply relaxed, with every single fiber in your body in a state of total rest.

8. Stay in this state for the next few minutes or as long as you'd like. If you are in bed, melt into the state and allow the sleep to come.

SELF-LOVE

We've all heard the saying "You can't love someone else unless you love your-self." But as many times as you've heard and reflected on that idea, how often do you *really* make the effort to deepen your love for yourself? I understand it can be challenging. But making time to appreciate, even celebrate, who you are, the life you lead, the relationships you maintain, the breaths you draw, the good decisions you make, and the body you nourish can be transformational. Rather than focus so much on your relationship with others, as we're all prone to do, in this meditation focus on yourself, without judgment, attachment, or fear. Doing so brings a powerful sense of peace that you can carry with you throughout your day or as you fall asleep at night. In fact, self-focus can be the best gift to give yourself at the end of a long day.

1. Find a comfortable seated position. You can sit cross-legged on a cushion on the floor or in a chair. Sit up straight, but don't force perfect posture.

2. Soften your gaze or gently close your eyes.

3. Take 5 deep breaths. Inhale slowly through your nose, and let out all the air through your mouth with an "ahhh" sound.

4. Allow your breath to return to its natural rhythm and stay with it for each inhale and exhale. Find and focus on a spot in your body where you feel your breath the most.

5. Bring your attention to the simplicity, purity, and peace of each breath. Your breath—your diaphragm contracting and relaxing, pulling air in and letting it out—is always there for you.

6. Bring your attention to your heart, beating softly and persistently in your chest, moving blood through your entire body to deliver nutrients and oxygen and remove toxins from every cell.

7. Bring your attention to your other internal organs, each dutifully doing its job to support the systems in your body.

8. Envision your endocrine and lymphatic systems creating hormones and fighting off invaders.

9. Bring your attention to your brain, connecting and processing signals from your entire body and the external world and providing the necessary information for you to move, act, and think.

10. Bring your attention to your muscles and your skin wrapping your body in protection. Consider your skeletal system, which provides the sturdy frame on which your entire body is assembled.

11. Consider your hair, the pigment of your skin, your eyes, your lips and mouth, your nose, the shape of your ears. This is you, 30 trillion to 40 trillion cells, perfectly arranged to make you *you*.

12. Take a moment to appreciate yourself for being who you are. You are the only version of you that there ever has been or ever will be. You are perfectly, completely alive. You are experiencing life right now.

13. When the meditation feels complete, bring your attention back to your breath for several cycles. Notice whether your awareness is heightened. Notice how each moment is brimming with novel experiences, some subtle, some bold. Remember that this ability to pay attention is always available to you. It will serve you well in daily life, and it can bring solace and peace if you're having trouble falling asleep.

BELLY FULL

The fact that our gut is lined with nearly 100 million neurons lends credibility to the old maxim "Go with your gut." You have likely experienced "butterflies in your stomach" or "a sinking feeling" or lack of hunger due to stress. You may have even experienced digestive issues related to stress, anxiety, or depression. Our digestive system is inextricably connected to every other system in our body and is deeply important to our overall health and sense of well-being. In this meditation, you will focus on the sensations in your belly and abdomen, bringing total awareness and relaxation to your digestive system, an area in which we often store stress. You might want to do this meditation after your evening meal to get the full effect.

1. Lie down on your back on a comfortable surface on the floor, such as a yoga mat or carpet, or on a bed or couch.

2. Soften your gaze or gently close your eyes.

3. Become aware of your breath. Take 5 deep breaths, focusing on the inhale and exhale. Let your breath return to its natural rhythm.

4. Identify a place in the cycle where you feel the sensation the most. It might be the tip of your nose, the bottom of your rib cage, or your belly. Focus on that sensation for the next several breaths. You can return to this sensation at any point in the meditation if you find you're becoming distracted by thoughts or external sounds or sensations.

5. Place your hands on your belly just below your rib cage. Feel the rise and fall of each breath for several breaths. Move your hands down to your lower abdomen and repeat for several breaths.

6. Remove your hands and let them relax at your sides.

7. Keeping your awareness on your belly, scan all the layers starting with your skin. Is it relaxed? Scan your abdominal muscles, the muscles on your sides, and your back. Are they completely relaxed? Try to relax them even more.

8. Bring your awareness to your stomach and your intestines. Are you storing stress or tension deep inside? Can you let it go?

9. Bring calm and total relaxation to this entire area until you feel total comfort and peace.

10. Connect to the gratitude you have for the food you've eaten and your body's system for processing it and delivering nutrition to your entire body.

11. You are full, warm, comfortable, and completely relaxed. You are in a state of rest.

CORPSE POSE

To someone who's new to yoga, the pose known as *Savasana*, or Corpse Pose, can look like little more than lying on your back, but it's all about what you bring to it. Usually offered at the end of a yoga session, Corpse Pose is restorative and optimal for a presleep meditation. In this meditation, you will use it to achieve deep relaxation of your full body and mind.

1. Begin by lying down on a comfortable surface, such as a yoga mat, carpet, or bed.

2. Soften your gaze or gently close your eyes. Take a long, slow inhale through your nose, and let all the air out through your mouth with an "ahhh" sound. Repeat 5 times.

3. Allow your breath to return to its natural rhythm. Don't try to change or control it. Just let it flow.

4. Become aware of the length of your body. Gently extend through your heels and through the top of your head, seeing if you can stretch yourself a little bit longer. Become aware of the length of your neck and of your whole spine. Become aware of the length of your upper arms and lower arms, each finger, and your entire hand. Become aware of the length and space between your shoulders and the top of your femurs. Move down through your legs and into your feet.

5. Feel the width of your body, the opposite sides of your head, and the distance from the outside of your left shoulder to the outside of your right shoulder. Feel the distance between your elbows, between your thumbs on each hand, and the space across your rib cage. Continue to move down through your body, considering the space and distance within the outermost edges of you.

6. Feel the depth of your body, from your forehead to the back of your head, from the tip of your chin to the back of your neck, from your sternum to your spine, from your abdomen to the sway in your lower back. Feel the depth from the top of your hip to the back of your glutes.

7. Feel the weight of your body and the pull of gravity on every cell.

8. Now let go of all thoughts. Focus on nothing, not even your breath. Just be completely relaxed and present for the rest of the meditation.

SUPINE COBBLER'S POSE

Supine Cobbler's Pose is a restorative yoga posture that most people find to be extremely relaxing. Although we tend to notice the tension we carry in our head, neck, back, and shoulders, we often don't notice some other areas of the body that carry stress. Sitting as much as we do, usually with our legs together, means that we may have much more stress in our hips and pelvic area than we realize. Supine Cobbler's Pose opens up the area of the body where the lower back, pelvis, and hips come together, gently stretching and relieving tension there. This meditation is great to do just before getting in bed.

NOTE: A gentle stretching or "opening" feeling is desirable in the Supine Cobbler's Pose. You should feel no pain or pinching. If you do, make any adjustments necessary to arrive at a position that is entirely relaxing.

1. Lie down on your back on a comfortable surface, such as a yoga mat, carpet, or bed. Place your hands by your hips, palms up.

2. Bring the soles of your feet together, letting your knees open apart as wide as possible. Your heels should be a comfortable distance from your pelvis. Find the place that works.

3. Most people will feel a nice stretch through the groin and deep into the hips.

4. Place a pillow, blanket, or yoga block under the outside of each knee so that you can completely relax your legs but still feel the slight stretch.

5. Once you have your knees supported, your heels together, and the rest of your body completely relaxed, take a few minutes to tune into your breath.

6. Notice whether you've developed any tension anywhere in the body, and give each area a full exhale to release it.

7. For the next several minutes, allow your breath to flow naturally, returning to it whenever you find your mind wandering.

8. Try to completely relax into the pose. Notice whether you feel occasional waves of release through your lower abdomen, groin muscles, hips, and lower back.

9. To come out of this pose, gently pull your knees toward your centerline. Bring your knees together and gently pull them toward your chest. Then place your feet on the bed or floor and stretch your legs out straight. Notice whether you feel a release in your hips, pelvis, and lower back.

10. Take a deep breath in through your nose, and exhale completely through your mouth. Repeat.

11. Gently move into a comfortable position and allow the feeling of relaxation to help carry you to sleep.

EVERYTHING IN PLACE

Much of our anxiety is associated with our desire to have control, for every-thing to be where and how we want it, for events to unfold in a manner consistent with our preferences, for people to behave how we'd like them to. In this meditation, as a way to wind down from the thinking and activities of the day, you're going to take some time to let go of your desire for order and control by reminding yourself that everything, in this very moment, is exactly where it is supposed to be—even if your house is messy.

1. After completing your nighttime routine, climb in bed for the night.

2. Reach your hands up toward the ceiling and very gently pull your head away from your body while dropping your shoulders down and away from your ears. Lower your hands back to your sides.

3. Soften your gaze or gently close your eyes.

4. Take in a deep breath, drawing air slowly through your nose. Hold your breath for a moment, then before exhaling, take one more sip of air through your nose. Completely fill your lungs. Pause for a moment.

5. Release all the air through your mouth with an "ahhh" sound, feeling all your stress and worry fall away as you do. Clear any remaining thoughts from your mind. Repeat 5 times.

6. Allow your breath to return to its natural rhythm. Find a place in your breath where the sensation is greatest and perhaps most pleasant. Focus on that place.

7. With your eyes closed and without moving, picture your body lying where it is. Notice how still and relaxed it appears. Scan your body to confirm that you actually are as relaxed as you appear.

8. Picture the room around you: the floor, the furniture, the walls, the windows. Moving systematically in one direction, scan all the items in the room. *Look through drawers and through the clothes in your closet.* Take care to not hurry. Spend as much time with each item as you'd like.

9. Continue moving through each room in your home, looking at the shelves, inside the cabinets, inside the fridge. Notice how everything is placed where you or a loved one put it, how each item tells a story of where it came from and how it got to where it is. Be conscious of not judging any item or wishing it to be different. You're merely observing where it is in your mind's eye, making note of its presence, location, shape, and form.

10. Everything is simply where it is, in its place, and its place is neither good nor bad. You are neutral, a passive observer. As you look at each item, avoid assigning any meaning, value, or judgment.

11. Consider how this practice is transferable to all aspects of life, how your interactions with people and sounds and sensations simply occur. These interactions are neither good nor bad on their own.

12. Slowly make your way back to your room. See yourself lying there, perfectly still and relaxed, alive and breathing.

13. You are, like everything else, in the only place you ever need to be: right where you are.

19

40 BREATHS 5 MINUTES

As you know by now, the breath is always an entry point into and an anchor throughout your meditation. It can also be the focus of the entire meditation, as this book has shown. In this meditation, you're going to take that concept further by focusing on 40 consecutive breaths, incrementally increasing their depth. This meditation is perfect before bedtime or naps because it quickly helps calm the nervous system and relax the body and mind.

1. Lie down on a comfortable surface, such as a yoga mat, carpet, or bed.

2. Take a moment to scan your body. Note areas of stress or tension and relax them.

3. Soften your gaze or gently close your eyes.

4. Feel the weight of your entire body sinking into the surface beneath you.

5. Take a slow, deep inhale through your nose. When you feel like your lungs are full, pause for moment, then take in a small extra sip of air.

6. As slowly as possible, exhale the air completely through your mouth. When you feel like you don't have any air left, pause for a moment, then gently push out the last remaining bit.

7. With each inhale, imagine you're breathing *in* peace, tranquility, calm, and relaxation.

8. With each exhale, imagine you're breathing *out* worry, tension, stress, anxiety, or pain.

9. Repeat this cycle for 40 breaths, counting at the end of each exhale.

10. Try to extend the length of the breath and the pauses at the end of each inhale and exhale. Avoid holding your breath or going so slowly that you feel you need to gasp for air.

11. Each breath should be completely managed in each moment. Remain present and focused on it.

12. If your mind wanders or an external sensation or sound pulls you away, return to your breath and resume the practice.

20

HEART OF GOLD 10 MINUTES

Whether or not you think of yourself as a "good person," I would bet that you have some amazing qualities that you tend to overlook. Cultural conditioning from a young age and other factors have given most of us a complicated view of ourselves. Our minds are very good at reminding us of our flaws, our short-comings, and our failures, and they are also very adept at presenting these thoughts as "truth." This tendency gives a false credibility to our thoughts and perpetuates our negative self-analysis. We can address this problem in two ways. One is to simply recognize that our thoughts are not automatically true. The other is to intentionally counteract negativity by proactively appreciating, celebrating, and loving ourselves for all of the good qualities that we possess. In this simple practice, you're going to remind yourself that you are alive, you are human, and you are good.

1. Find a comfortable seated position. You can sit cross-legged on a cushion on the floor or in a chair. Sit up straight, but don't force perfect posture.

2. Soften your gaze or gently close your eyes.

3. Take a deep breath. Repeat 3 times.

4. Return your breath to its natural rhythm and bring your focus to a particular sensation in the cycle of your breathing.

5. Allow any remaining thoughts, worries, or preoccupations to drift away. You have nowhere else to be and nothing else to do. You are here, in this moment, alive, aware, breathing.

6. Either in your mind or speaking softly out loud, repeat the following: *I am alive. I am aware. I am good.* Let the weight and meaning of each word resonate. Say each word with focus and intention.

7. Continue to repeat the words at a slow, consistent rhythm.

8. Return your focus to your breath should you find your mind has wandered or become distracted.

The repeated words in this meditation are available to you anytime. You may find them especially comforting when you're lying in bed preparing for sleep.

TIP: Be nice to yourself. Treat yourself with love and compassion. Let go of thought patterns that aren't serving you. Appreciate the amazing richness of this moment. You are alive. You are aware. You are good.

Resources

For a list of audio tracks, videos, and other helpful resources, please visit yfm.tv/bookresources.

Awareness: Conversations with the Masters by Anthony De Mello

Lovingkindness: The Revolutionary Art of Happiness by Sharon Salzberg

Radical Acceptance: Embracing Your Life with the Heart of a Buddha by Tara Brach

The Power of Now: A Guide to Spiritual Enlightenment by Eckhart Tolle

Waking Up: A Guide to Spirituality Without Religion by Sam Harris

Wherever You Go, There You Are: Mindfulness Meditation in Everyday Life by Jon Kabat-Zinn

Headspace
Simple, straightforward meditation instruction from Andy Puddicombe, a former Buddhist monk turned meditation teacher and tech entrepreneur. The app offers 10 free meditations before you pay for a subscription.

Waking Up
Insightful meditation practices from neuroscientist, philosopher, and meditation teacher Sam Harris. The practices are deep and powerful. The app offers five free meditations before you pay for a subscription.

References

ScienceDaily (blog). "Inadequate Sleep Could Cost Countries Billions." June 4, 2018. Accessed February 27, 2019. https://www.sciencedaily.com /releases/2018/06/180604093111.htm.

Stress Reduction

Goyal, Madhav, Sonal Singh, Erica Sibinga, Neda F. Gould, Anastasia Rowland-Seymour, Ritu Sharma, Zackary Berger, Dana Sleicher, David D. Maron, Hasan M. Shihab, Padmini D. Ranasinghe, Shauna Linn, Shonali Saha, Eric B. Bass, and Jennifer A. Haythornthwaite. "Meditation Programs for Psychological Stress and Well-being." *JAMA Internal Medicine* 174, no. 3 (2014): 357-68. doi:10.1001/jamainternmed.2013.13018. https://www.ncbi.nlm.nih .gov/pubmed/24395196.

Orme-Johnson, David W., and Vernon A. Barnes. "Effects of the Transcendental Meditation Technique on Trait Anxiety: A Meta-Analysis of Randomized Controlled Trials." *Journal of Alternative and Complementary Medicine* 20, no. 5 (2014): 330-41. doi:10.1089/acm.2013.0204. https://www.ncbi.nlm.nih .gov/pubmed/24107199.

Rosenkranz, Melissa A., Richard J. Davidson, Donal G. MacCoon, John F. Sheridan, Ned H. Kalin, and Antoine Lutz. "A Comparison of Mindfulness-Based Stress Reduction and an Active Control in Modulation of Neurogenic Inflammation." *Brain, Behavior, and Immunity* 27 (2013): 174-84. doi:10.1016 /j.bbi.2012.10.013. https://www.sciencedirect.com/science/article/pii /S0889159112004758.

Improved Sleep

EOC Institute. "Meditation vs Sleep: 5 Reasons Meditation Replaces Your Sleep." Accessed February 27, 2019. https://eocinstitute.org/meditation/require-less-sleep-with-meditation-460/.

Martires, Joanne, and Michelle Zeidler. "The Value of Mindfulness Meditation in the Treatment of Insomnia." *Current Opinion in Pulmonary Medicine* 21, no. 6 (2015): 547-52. doi:10.1097/mcp.0000000000000207.

Nagendra, Ravindra P., Nirmala Maruthai, and Bindu M. Kutty. "Meditation and Its Regulatory Role on Sleep." *Frontiers in Neurology* 3 (2012). doi:10.3389/fneur.2012.00054.

Reduced Blood Pressure

Levine, Glenn N., Richard A. Lange, C. Noel Bairey-Merz, Richard J. Davidson, Kenneth Jamerson, Puja K. Mehta, Erin D. Michos, Keith Norris, Indranill Basu Ray, Karen L. Saban, Tina Shah, Richard Stein, Sidney C. Smith Jr, and the American Heart Association Council on Clinical Cardiology; Council on Cardiovascular and Stroke Nursing; and Council on Hypertension. "Meditation and Cardiovascular Risk Reduction: A Scientific Statement from the American Heart Association." *Journal of the American Heart Association* 6, no. 10 (2017). doi:10.1161/jaha.117.002218.

Principles of Meditation

Fletcher, Emily. "What's the Difference between Mindfulness and Meditation?" *Mindbodygreen*. October 13, 2017. Accessed February 27, 2019. https://www.mindbodygreen.com/0-27292/whats-the-difference-between-mindfulness-meditation.html.

Om Swami (blog). "Six Principles of Meditation." March 14, 2017. Accessed February 27, 2019. http://omswami.com/2014/05/six -principles-of-meditation.html.

PsychAlive. YouTube. January 03, 2013. Accessed February 27, 2019. https://www.youtube.com/watch?v=HmEo6RI4Wvs.

MBSR

Ackerman, Courtney. "MBSR: 25 Mindfulness-based Stress Reduction Exercises and Courses." Positive Psychology Program—Your One-Stop PP Resource! January 10, 2019. Accessed February 23, 2019. https:// positivepsychologyprogram.com/mindfulness-based-stress -reduction-mbsr/.

"History of MBSR." University of Massachusetts Medical School. November 17, 2016. Accessed February 28, 2019. https://www.umassmed .edu/cfm/mindfulness-based-programs/mbsr-courses/about-mbsr /history-of-mbsr/.

MBCT

Mindfulness-Based Cognitive Therapy. "About MBCT." Accessed February 23, 2019. http://www.mbct.com/.

Types of Meditation

Gaiam (blog). "Meditation 101: Techniques, Benefits, and a Beginner's How-to." Accessed February 23, 2019. https://www.gaiam.com/blogs/discover /meditation-101-techniques-benefits-and-a-beginner-s-how-to.

Lechner, Tamara. "5 Types of Meditation Decoded." *The Chopra Center* (blog). March 2, 2018. Accessed February 23, 2019. https://chopra.com/articles/5-types-of-meditation-decoded.

Sockolov, Matthew. "17 Types of Meditation—Which One Is for You?" One Mind Dharma. December 11, 2018. Accessed February 23, 2019. https://oneminddharma.com/types-of-meditation/.

Welch, Ashley. "A Guide to 7 Different Types of Meditation | Everyday Health." EverydayHealth.com (blog). June 22, 2018. Accessed February 23, 2019. https://www.everydayhealth.com/meditation/types/.

PRACTICES

Deep Belly Breaths

Yogapedia.com (blog). "What Is Pranayama? Definition from Yogapedia." Accessed February 23, 2019. https://www.yogapedia.com/definition/4990/pranayama.

Belly Full

Underwood, Emily. "Your Gut Is Directly Connected to Your Brain, by a Newly Discovered Neuron Circuit." *Science | AAAS*. September 20, 2018. Accessed February 23, 2019. https://www.sciencemag.org/news/2018/09/your-gut-directly-connected-your-brain-newly-discovered-neuron-circuit.

Index

Acceptance, 7
Affirmations, 12
Alternate Reality, 70–71
Anxiety, 42–43, 138–139
Appreciation, 24–25, 70–71
Aromatherapy, 40–41, 112–113
Awareness, 4, 7

Baths, 56–57
Bed in the Forest, 106–107
Belly Full, 132–133
Birthday Suit, 126–127
Blood pressure, 4
Brach, Tara, 76
Breathing, 114–115, 140–141
Bukowski, Charles, 100

Candle Flame, 28–29
Chanting, 13
Child's Pose, 72–73
Chimes, 94–95
Classic Reset, The, 20–21
Comfort, 122–123
Compassion, 8, 142–143
Concentration, 12
Confidence, 86–87
Control, 138–139
Corpse Pose, 134–135
Cup of Tea, A, 112–113

Deep Belly Breaths, 114–115
Digestive system, 132–133
Dinner Party, 116–117
Don't Keep Going, 88–89

Emotions, 50–51, 76–77
Equanimity, 4
Everything in Place, 138–139
Expert in Being You, 86–87
Eye of the Storm, 64–65

Feeling Your Feelings, 50–51
Finding Silence, 118–119
Floating, 124–125
Focal points, 28–29, 34–35,
    78–79
Focus, 12
Forgiveness, 8, 90–91
40 Breaths, 140–141
Found Sound, 74–75
Frenemy, 80–81
Frustration, 17
Full of Gratitude, 98–99
Full of Light, 62–63

Generosity, 84–85
Get Comfortable, 122–123
Getting Real, 82–83
Give It Away, 84–85
Gratitude, 98–99
Gravity, 106–107

Happiness, 76–77
Heart of Gold, 142–143

Kabat-Zinn, Jon, 7, 10–11
Kaminoff, Leslie, 74

Laughing Heart, The, 100–101
Light as Light, 120–121

Meditation
    benefits of, 2–4
    principles of, 7–9
    and thoughts, 5–6
    tips, 14–17
    types of, 12–13
    what it is not, 6
Melatonin, 3
Mindfulness, 4, 12
Mindfulness-based cognitive therapy
        (MBCT), 11
Mindfulness-based stress reduction
        (MBSR), 10
Music, 30–31

Nakedness, 126–127
Nonattachment, 9, 44–45, 46–47
Nonjudgmental awareness, 7
Nonstriving, 9, 46–47, 48–49
No Worries, 48–49

Object of Desire, 44–45
Om, 32–33
"Over-stress, under-rest" cycle, 2

Pain, 64–65
Past, letting go of, 24–25
Patience, 7
Pausing, 88–89
People Everywhere, 42–43
Perspective, 26–27, 78–79, 92–93,
        104–105, 110–111
Pet Tonic, 36–37

Phrases, 12
Pinnacle, 104–105
Poetry, 100–101
Posture, 68–69
Pranayama, 114–115
Present and Complete, 22–23
Present moment, 6, 22–23, 104–105

Rainfall, 38–39
Relationships, 80–81, 90–91
Relaxation, 2–4, 19, 128–129, 134–135

Satellite Vision, 110–111
Savasana, 134–135
Segal, Zindel, 11
Self-Love, 130–131
Silence, 118–119
Sleep, 3, 103
Smell, sense of, 40–41, 112–113
Smile Like Your Life Depends on It, 76–77
Smooth Tunes, 30–31
"Softening your gaze," 21
Sound of Om, The, 32–33
Sounds, 38–39, 74–75, 94–95, 124–125
Stress reduction, 3–4, 61
Super Thoughts, 66–67
Supine Cobbler's Pose, 136–137

Teasdale, John, 11
Temperature, 108–109
Thoughts, 5, 66–67, 120–121, 142–143
Tiny Walk, A, 78–79
Tonglen, 13
Tonus Dissolver, 128–129
Top of the World, 58–59
Triggers, 4
Trust, 8, 52–53, 54–55
Two Inches Taller, 68–69

Vipassana, 12
Visualization, 11, 58–59, 62–63,
    116–117, 124–125

Walking meditations, 26–27, 96–97
Walk in the Woods, A, 96–97
Wallflower, 34–35
Wanting Nothing, 46–47
Warm Feet, Cool Head, 108–109
Water Pressure, 56–57
Weightless, 26–27

Weil, Andrew, 56
What Truly Matters, 92–93
Williams, Mark, 11
Worrying, 48–49

Yoga, 72–73, 114–115, 134–137
You are Trustworthy, 54–55
You Can't Take It with You, 24–25

Ziglar, Zig, 70

Acknowledgments

A special thank you to my mom, Beckie O'Neill, for bringing the wisdom of yoga and meditation to our family for all of these years. I simply would not have been able to write this book without the invaluable insights you've shared throughout my entire life. Thanks for inspiring us to be ambitious and confident (and to have the audacity to do things like write books!). Writing this guide to meditation brought me closer to you, to so many of the things you say, and to your way of being in the world, and it gave me a renewed respect and appreciation for what you've been trying to tell us for so long. I love you. Thank you . . . for everything.

To my incredibly supportive, smart, funny, beautiful, and loving wife, Anya: Thank you for the countless compromises you make. I marvel at you. I am so grateful for you. I love you *this* much.

To my friend and business partner, Robert "Sunshine" Sidoti: Thanks for all the two-and-a-half-hour-one-way commutes, the crashing on the couch, the travel. Thanks for creating those amazing classes that bring strength and growth to so many lives and for sticking it out all these years. This book would not have happened were it not for the decade-long journey we've shared. Thanks for doing what you do, the way you do it.

About the Author

Adam O'Neill is the CEO of YFM.tv, a company born from the merger of Broga® Yoga (which he cofounded) and Yoga for Men. YFM is an abbreviation of "Yoga. Fitness. Mindfulness." Adam lives on a small farm in central New York with his wife, Anya, daughter, Maeve, and their dog, cat, goats, and chickens.

CPSIA information can be obtained
at www.ICGtesting.com
Printed in the USA
BVHW061141220419
546170BV00008B/9/P

9 781641 523950